LEADING CHANGE

The Case for Continuous Improvement

Katheryn W. Gemberling
Carl W. Smith
Joseph S. Villani

Case Studies Judith Brody Saks

The Key Work of School Boards Series
National School Boards Association
Alexandria, Virginia

ISBN 0-88364-278-6

1680 Duke St.
Alexandria, VA 22314
703- 838-6722
www.nsba.org

Cover Design by Brian Gallagher
Page Design and Production by Stephanie Wikberg

CONTENTS

FOREWORD

"Every day in every way, we're getting better and better." That old self-improvement mantra, meant to be repeated in front of the mirror each morning, takes on new meaning for school leaders who are committed to continuous improvement.

A foundational aspect of the Key Work of School Boards model, continuous improvement is not just another set of management tools. It is a way of thinking about everything we do and seeking ways to do it better. It is a habit of mind that brings a different perspective to an organization—a perspective rooted in data and preoccupied with quality.

To help school boards cultivate and reinforce this thoughtful and reflective habit of mind, the National School Boards Association has developed *Leading Change: The Case for Continuous Improvement*. This new title in NSBA's Key Work of School Boards series explores the elements of continuous improvement and provides scenarios, self-assessments, and questions boards can ask to gauge their understanding and application of these concepts.

Also included are case studies of three school districts that are using continuous improvement to question, examine, revise, refine, and revisit what they do and how they do it. Constantly adapting, these districts are well on the way to becoming what Peter Senge calls "learning organizations."

Continuous improvement, the authors of *Leading Change* write, is a journey, not a destination. As you and your district embark on this journey, we hope you'll find this book a useful road map.

Anne L. Bryant
Executive Director
National School Boards Association

INTRODUCTION

CONTINUOUS IMPROVEMENT:
A CRITICAL CONCEPT FOR SCHOOL BOARDS

Continuous improvement is a deceptively simple concept to grasp. But as with many commonsense notions, it is easier to understand than it is to practice. Why is this so? In *The Key Work of School Boards Guidebook*, continuous improvement is described as a "habit of mind," and it is helpful to begin this discussion by returning to that notion.

Most of us are familiar with paradigms in the context of systems thinking, but a brief reintroduction to this concept for discussion purposes is useful. Another way of looking at paradigms is as mental models—pictures in our minds. These mental models are formed by our experiences. They provide lenses for viewing the world and making sense of events. And they have a cultural context. Paradigms are useful in providing road maps for solving problems successfully. We all tend to solve problems by drawing on past experience.

A major problem with paradigms is that they condition the way we see events and cause us to zero in on information and reinforce attitudes that conform to our existing points of view. At one level, doing so is very useful; at another level, this selectivity may blind us to other ways of seeing and solving problems, in short, of making sense of our world. Joel Barker referred to this phenomenon as "paradigm paralysis." If the event that you are trying to make sense of does not fit your paradigm, there is a good chance you will be blinded to other ways of thinking and solving problems.

It is a very real challenge for us to reach beyond our paradigms. A Native American adage says you cannot understand another person until you have walked five miles in that person's moccasins. In their useful book *Reframing Organizations*, Terrence Deal and Lee Bolman provide a series of lenses for viewing the same organization and the same events.

How does any of this apply to continuous improvement as a habit of mind? Continuous improvement begins by questioning, not in a critical but in an inquiring way, what we are doing and how we are doing it. Sometimes, such questions can even lead us back to why we are doing what we have been doing. Most often the questioning begins when we get a result that is disappointing, well below what we expected. It is at those moments that we have a choice. We can direct that everyone work harder on solving the problem and return only when it is solved. Or, we can begin asking more questions.

Let us suppose a new reading program has been instituted with high hopes and expectations for improving students' reading skills. When the board receives the testing results from the first year, the scores show some modest improvement but not enough to be statistically significant. What should the board do? If the board's frame of reference is to solve problems—to find out why the results are disappointing, to probe beneath the surface—the board is moving in the direction of continuous improvement. Perhaps in this instance, the board discovers that the in-service training for teachers was delayed because of budget problems and not completed until well into the second semester. Perhaps other issues surface as well. Armed with new information, the board can take steps to provide the resources and authority to address the identified impediments to progress.

But the process does not stop there. Let us suppose that the next time the board receives test results, significant progress is evident. The board uses that moment to celebrate the forward progress and commend those responsible. At the same time, the board continues to home in on the essential continuous improvement question: What can we do now to get even better results in the next go-round? When the first action is coupled with the second action, the board is practicing continuous improvement.

Keep in mind that it is not the board's job to go forth and take direct action to improve reading performance. The board's responsibility is to approach issues from a problem-solving, rather than a finger-pointing, perspective. It is the board's job to ask the right questions, identify the data it needs to measure progress, and respond to staff recommendations regarding actions to be taken and changes to be made. It is the board's role to model what it expects and to create a culture in the school system that values open, honest discussion and focuses not on how badly a program is doing, but how much better it could be.

Of course, it is easy to make hypothetical scenarios come out the way you want them to. Sometimes, even after several tries, the board may decide to scrap a program or call for its radical reorganization. That is not the point. The point here is that practicing continuous improvement means being willing to reach beyond present ways of thinking to develop new paradigms, new ways of solving problems, better ways of framing issues.

An important early step on the journey to continuous improvement is to develop a *customer focus* that guides and informs the decisions of the board and the staff. W. Edwards Deming believed that two questions best capture the notion of customer: Whom do I serve? And, who serves me? Applied to the external customer, such an approach means that effective school systems spend considerable time understanding who they serve and what those customers want. This means substantive and sustained community engagement. It means really listening to parents, students, and business and other community leaders and responding to what they say. There are many ways to engage the community, and we will talk about some of them in later sections of this book.

Having a customer focus applies to teachers, principals, and staff members and to the board and superintendent. Within the system, it is important for all staff members to know clearly who their customers are. We all have many customers. The fourth-grade teacher, for example, is a customer of the third-grade teacher, who must know what the school system and receiving teacher expect of students and prepare them accordingly. The third-grade teacher also needs feedback from the fourth-grade teacher about where the students were proficient and where they were not. And on it goes, permeating the organization.

It is useful for a board to hold a session to examine who its customers are. If the session is far-reaching, some very interesting conversation is likely to ensue. Some customers, such as parents, are obvious, but others are less so. For example, most teachers who retire elect to remain in the communities where they have lived and taught. Are they customers of the school system? What do they think about the board's priorities? How do they influence others' thinking about the school system? In truth, the board has many customers and many voices to attend to. Developing awareness of who the board's customers are and establishing paths of communication to and for them is a critical first step in practicing continuous improvement.

Another essential challenge for any board that is committed to continuous improvement is to create a climate in the school system that values continuous improvement and to reward those who practice it. This book does not provide 10 easy steps for doing so. We have learned that in education, as in other enterprises, prescriptions and cookie-cutter approaches simply do not work. Each school system is unique, with its own history, culture, and priorities. Creating a climate in the district office and in local schools in which continuous improvement is valued and practiced will require actions tailored to the district's circumstances. A good two-part question to begin with is, How can we create the conditions in our school district that foster risk-taking and promote data-driven decision making?

The first part of this question is about culture. In too many school districts, the messages to staff at all levels come from the top down. When that is the prevailing norm, people do not take risks; they do what they are directed to do. They are more likely to end up complying with the directions of their superiors even when they disagree. Although they may actually resent having to comply and may take little responsibility for results, if that is the way the system operates, they will go along. Any effort to promote continuous improvement in such a system will likely fail. Staff members are more likely to take ownership and participate when a school system aligns authority with responsibility and encourages input and involvement. That involvement has to be substantive, not pro forma. When it is substantive and individuals believe that their ideas count and are respected, the foundation for continuous improvement is in place.

The second part of the question focuses on data and the use of data to make decisions. A quip that applies here is, "In God we trust—all others bring data." Continuous improvement is not just about data, but in the absence of data, efforts to improve will as often miss the mark as hit the mark. It is a little like trying to play a basketball game with the scoreboard turned off. Data implies analysis. When a problem arises, many people will offer solutions based on their past experience. The problem is that the circumstances of the past never precisely mirror the circumstances of the present; put another way, what worked in the past may or may not work in the present or in the future.

The first step in continuous improvement, then, is analysis of the problem: What is the problem? How do we know? The next challenge is to devise strategies for resolving the issues uncovered and take actions based on those strategies. The third step is to monitor progress and make adjustments as needed to ensure progress toward the goal. Finally, this problem-solving cycle needs to become an integral part of the work of the board and the staff in all aspects of the operation.

The last point is particularly important. Continuous improvement, not sporadic improvement, is the goal. Continuous improvement is about fixing things before they are broken. It is about finding better, more efficient ways to operate that promote continuous progress. It is about never resting on one's laurels.

A second essential challenge for boards who elect to promote continuous improvement is to model what they expect from others in the school system. Too often, there is a disconnect between what we espouse and what we actually do. It is not enough for a board to promote continuous improvement for everyone except the board. Boards must ask similar question of themselves as they have asked of others. How do we as a board create the conditions that will enable us to take actions that are consistent with our expectations of others? Do we look critically at our meetings and in other ways assess our effectiveness as a board? How and how consistently do we use data to make decisions? For example, it does little good for a board to tell the staff that it encourages open discussion and the free interplay of ideas at the same time as individual board members advance personal agendas, network with staff in divisive ways, launch personnel attacks on their colleagues, and ignore the data that support a recommended action. Continuous improvement, like many other things, begins at home.

In the remaining chapters of this book, we will have a chance to probe more deeply into the issues raised in this introduction:

- What strategies and processes can boards use to promote continuous improvement throughout their school systems?
- What strategies have other boards used to model continuous improvement?
- Where is this work being done well?
- What have been the results?

CHAPTER 1

BEGINNING WITH THE END IN MIND

What does it mean to *begin with the end in mind*? It means determining desired outcomes before taking action. One of Stephen Covey's seven habits of highly effective people is to *begin with the end in mind*. You may recall *Alice in Wonderland*'s Cheshire Cat telling Alice that if she did not know where she was going, any of the roads before her would do. But if we have to be in a particular place at a point in time, then any road will not do. We may have more than one road to take, but the choice of roads cannot be random. How many of us would take an important trip with only a rough idea of where we wanted to go or how we would get there? Arriving at our destination requires a plan.

In continuous improvement, it is essential to *begin with the end in mind*. That means, among other things, determining and communicating the vision, mission, and desired outcomes for the school system. If we continue the trip analogy, *beginning with the end in mind* is about the destination. Continuous improvement is the journey itself.

How the board determines the destination is as important as the destination itself. Before the first step of the journey is taken, before the first road map is examined, the board must decide where it wants to go and why. One of the best ways to get at the where and why is for board members to ask a simple question: At the end of our term in office, what is our legacy to the district? Continuing Covey's analogy, consider this a eulogy of sorts. What will we be remembered for? In what direction did we take this district? What was the biggest obstacle to excellence we faced? How did we set targets to eliminate that block? What was our goal? How close did we come? What was our specific contribution? Did we make a difference?

The answers to such questions require a specific role for school boards—leadership rather than management. Answering these questions may challenge existing practices and long-standing ways of thinking and operating. A school board engaged in continuous improvement is a leadership group unafraid to challenge existing norms, standards, and behaviors. The board members deviate from the ongoing journey begun by prior leaders to examine first whether the current destination is still viable. They revisit the practices that got them to where they are now and realistically question themselves as to whether these practices can take them where they need to go. They exercise *leadership* rather than *followership*. We'll examine this concept in more detail in Chapter 6, "Leading by Example." Leadership is critical in choosing the direction of the school district, though it may be difficult to change course after so many years of continuing along a well-worn path. The only difference between a well-worn path, a rut, and a grave is the depth.

In continuous improvement, process and product are interconnected. Charting the course for the school system requires more than happenstance. The board needs to know not only where it wants to go but also where it is. The first step is a needs analysis, sometimes referred to as scanning the environment. The board must know how well the system is achieving its present mission and goals. For example, how well are students doing on state and locally mandated tests? How many students graduate? How many go on successfully to college? Are the answers to these questions consistent for all groups of students? How are resource allocations supporting the mission? What do parents, students, and community leaders really expect of the schools? Most important, what evidence does the board currently gather that enables it to answer these questions? The critical point here is to determine where the system is now.

The next step is to decide what the board intends the system to accomplish and how—in other words, to set the destination. Let's use the journey analogy again. Suppose you've been on the road to New York from Washington, D.C. You've traveled along a route that previous leaders believed would get you there at a certain time. But you're not there yet. In fact, you're only in Philadelphia. The question now is not how you can get to New York more quickly. The question to ask yourself at this point is: Do we still need to go to New York—or even want to? Is New York the best place for us? Would it be better to go to Boston or Chicago? Why choose one over the other? What do we want our end destination to be?

This part of the process needs to be collaborative. The board cannot retreat to a mountaintop and, after a period of reflection, announce what the school system will accomplish and how. Covey reminds us that where there has been no engagement, there will be little commitment—compliance perhaps, but not commitment. Moreover, engaging the staff and the community in conversations about the vision, mission, and goals of the system will give the board invaluable information about issues, needs, and expectations. Robust community engagement is central to the Key Work model for board leadership.

At another level, *beginning with the end in mind* requires that we answer the question: How will we know when we're there? This means spelling out in objective terms what the desired results will look like and what data the board will need to measure those results. Agreement on the data up front is critical to sustaining continuous improvement. Without data, the board will not be able to decide what is working and what is not working. The essential challenge for the board will be to determine which of the actions taken have added sufficient value and which have not. In the language of systems thinking, the board is looking for opportunities for improvement. This may mean modifying or adding to existing plans, maintaining the status quo, or eliminating some programs and initiatives. Making the tough decisions is essential to promoting and sustaining a culture that is focused on performance and results. *Beginning with the end in mind* begins at the beginning.

The Baldrige National Quality Program, administered by the National Institute for Standards and Technology, is a useful resource for boards of education and school districts pursuing the goals of quality and continuous improvement. It identifies the key elements of effective organizations and provides a framework for assessing strengths and opportunities for improvement. The criteria are grouped into seven major categories, and points are awarded for each based on the review. The greatest weight in terms of possible points to be awarded is reserved for results, category seven, where an organization can earn 450 out of a possible 1,000 points. The message is clear—no matter what is intended, the final measure of district effectiveness is results.

The emphasis on results in the Baldrige program highlights the importance of using data as feedback and guide. Continuous improvement is ultimately data driven. Imagine playing an entire basketball game without a scoreboard and only turning the scoreboard on after the last whistle to see who won. No serious game could be held under such conditions, yet too often school districts operate in exactly that way. The academic year proceeds, standardized tests are given as required in late spring, and almost no one knows how well the district, schools, and students performed until the school year is over or nearly over. Continuous improvement thrives on data. Gathering data about how well individual units and the district itself are doing is the responsibility of everyone, most especially the board.

To do its job well, the board and staff must have ongoing information about how well the system is performing and the results it is getting. Multiple sources of evidence must be gathered at regular intervals during the school year. Evidence must be collected for individual students, classrooms, grades, and schools and for the district as a whole. Most importantly, data must be in a useful format for decision making.

Boards cannot be intimidated by the data game. Without timely and useful data, the board has little basis for intervening to improve performance or achieve the system's goals. The district that uses ongoing data collection and analysis should experience no surprises at high-stakes testing time. The external assessment should confirm for the public what the board and staff already know. Waiting for external data to determine success is fruitless.

"Data" is broadly defined in the continuous improvement model. Student results are clearly the endgame, but student performance data is not the only data boards should collect. It isn't enough to know student results. The board must determine how effective their own decisions are. Did we spend our money wisely? Do we have the right staff in the right places? Is the training we provide for staff making a difference for students? Did our investment pay off? Are our system operations cost effective? How satisfied are our parents and our students? How well are we serving our community?

The responsibilities of the board do not end here; deciding how to make the journey is the next challenge. Many intermediate steps will be needed to ensure alignment of resources, to promote process improvement, and to make key adjustments based on the experience of staff and students. These responsibilities will be discussed in subsequent chapters.

In summary, *beginning with the end in mind* means knowing where you're going and how you'll know when you've arrived before deciding how to get there. In the beginning and in the end, the main thing is still the main thing.

Scenario: Beginning with the End in Mind

The district is concerned about its inability to close the achievement gap among racial and ethnic groups on SAT math scores. Five years ago district leaders set the goal of eliminating this gap. The board approved the following initiatives:

- Students with lower math performance were placed in remedial classes.
- SAT test-prep courses were established in all high schools.
- Counselors met with groups of underachieving students to encourage them to do better.
- Letters were sent to all parents requesting them to encourage their students to take the SATs.
- All math teachers were given diversity training.
- All teachers were encouraged to use mathematics computation examples in their own content areas.
- Warm-up problems were required weekly.

After five years of these interventions, the data is decidedly disappointing. Not only is the gap not eliminated, it is not even reduced. In fact, the gap appears to be widening. Where does the board go now?

Faced with this scenario, a board might decide that the district has done all it can do. It is time to set new goals and undertake new initiatives that provide a better return on investment.

But a board that is willing to practice continuous improvement will take a different approach. It will seek answers to questions such as the following:

- Should we keep this goal?
- Is this goal consistent with our vision and mission?
- Is this goal important to delivering on our mission?
- What will happen if we don't stay the course?
- Who are the children we are willing to give up on?

The board must reflect on its goals. Failure to reach a goal is not a reason to change the target. Continuous improvement provides a framework for reexamining goals. If the board members still believe in the goal, they must reaffirm their commitment to it. Most importantly, continuous improvement opens the door to new and different ways ultimately to achieve the goal.

Keep this scenario in mind as you proceed through the next chapters. We will return to this discussion as we examine other elements of continuous improvement.

Self-Assessment

To what degree has your board/district achieved the following elements for beginning with the end in mind?

	Fully Achieved	Mostly Achieved	Partially Achieved	Beginning to Achieve
We begin with the end in mind.	❏	❏	❏	❏
We engage the community in identifying the outcomes for K-12 education.	❏	❏	❏	❏
We revisit our goals to ensure that they are still the correct targets.	❏	❏	❏	❏
We reflect frequently on how well we are leading the organization to reach our destination.	❏	❏	❏	❏
We challenge existing practices as well as our own decisions to achieve our end goal.	❏	❏	❏	❏
We follow the old carpenter's adage: measure twice, cut once.	❏	❏	❏	❏
We regularly monitor stakeholder satisfaction and dissatisfaction.	❏	❏	❏	❏
We clearly define the way we will determine success on our key priorities.	❏	❏	❏	❏
We have identified what measures we will use to determine progress toward our goals.	❏	❏	❏	❏
We have identified what measures we will use as evidence of attainment of our goals.	❏	❏	❏	❏

Use this self-assessment tool both to get started and to monitor your progress on the continuous improvement journey. Initial assessments may change as your progress and understanding grow.

Questions for Boards to Ask

How do we determine our end results?
- How does the district define the vision, mission, and goals that are aligned with current requirements and expectations?
- How has the board defined and communicated specific targets and end results that will measure success?
- What interim measures does the district define that determine progress toward our goals?
- How do we know what these measures are?
- What are the measures that we need but that are not available to us?
- How often do we review our mission and goals to determine if they are still the appropriate targets?
- What role do external forces such as state and federal mandates play in determining our end results?

How do we engage all key stakeholders in determining our mission and goals?
- What role does staff play in developing our mission and goals?
- How do we engage all levels of staff in creating the mission and goals?
- How do we create commitment rather than compliance?
- What role do our employee organizations play in developing our mission and goals?
- How do we engage the community in determining our end results?
- How do we ensure that all subgroups within our community are represented in choosing our mission and goals?
- When do we exert our own leadership in guiding the mission and goals?
- How do we hold ourselves responsible for setting the destination?

Are we willing to confront the tough issues?
- How do we respond to bad news?
- Who do we blame when we fail to reach our desired end results?
- What's the evidence that we are willing to chart a new and different course?
- What's the evidence that we are willing to challenge established norms and power structures?
- What's the evidence that our school district is more attuned to the needs of children than the needs of adults?
- What's the evidence that we are willing to challenge existing paradigms as we strive to accomplish our mission and goals?
- What's the evidence that we are politically brave?

- How have we shown that we are willing to take on the sacred cows that are no longer productive and need to be put to pasture?
- What's the evidence that we focus more on doing things the right way or on doing the right things?

References

Baldrige National Quality Program, www.baldrige.nist.gov.
Covey, Stephen R. *The Seven Habits of Highly Effective People: Restoring the Character Ethic.* Simon and Schuster, 1989.

CHAPTER 2

BUILDING THE INFORMATION FOUNDATION

Building an information foundation is essential to becoming a continuous improvement organization. What does that mean? What is an information foundation, and why do we need one? How do we build one for our district? What steps should we as board members take to make this happen?

Underpinning continuous improvement and systems thinking is the assumption that decision making in the organization is based on facts and focus, rather than perceptions and politics. If we examine how our own school districts operate, we might find that the tradition of political influence and public perceptions have guided most of our decisions. These practices were understandable when board members had little or no access to well-founded data to provide them with sufficient facts. In today's Information Age, however, lack of access to data is inexcusable. Consequently, board members need to revisit how we make our decisions and, more importantly, how we evaluate the results of those decisions.

What Do We Need To Know To Build an Information Foundation?

It is not necessary to become a statistics genius or computer whiz in order to make data-driven decisions. In fact, the purpose of a strong information foundation is to make data available quickly, easily, and in user-friendly formats. Data should be easy to interpret and easy to explain to others. With state test data being made available to the community through various public websites, parents and others are doing their own analyses and drawing their own conclusions about the success of schools. School districts must have the capacity to analyze and present their own data efficiently and effectively. They must be able to tell their story through facts, rather than anecdotes.

Ask yourselves the following questions:
- Do we receive data that is timely?
- Is the data provided in a user-friendly format?
- Do we discuss the data openly?
- Do we use the data to inform our decisions?
- Do we gather evidence to determine whether our policies are being implemented?
- Do we gather evidence about the impact of our policy decisions?
- Do we have the infrastructure in place to store, access, analyze, and report all the data we need to guide our decision making?

Few districts can answer *yes* to all these questions. Many may not answer *yes* to most of them. The accountability requirements of No Child Left Behind (NCLB) are changing how school boards and school district leaders must react in a data-laden environment. Having a purposeful and effective data structure for school districts is neither a luxury nor an option. Building an information foundation is essential for survival in this era of public accountability. Understanding how to use this information foundation to guide and review decision making is at the core of becoming a continuous improvement organization.

What Data Basics Should Boards Know To Build an Information Foundation?

A picture is worth a thousand words. Board members already receive thousands of pages of data each year, and NCLB is no doubt increasing the data load. Poring through reams of tables and number charts can be confusing and frustrating. Data should be represented in graphic format whenever possible. Graphs make comparisons more immediately evident. There are multiple types of graphs and charts, each with its own purpose and information. Board members should become familiar not only with the simpler types of chart, such as bar graphs, column graphs, and pie charts, but also with the more sophisticated types, such as stacked columns, scatter plots, and box-and-whisker plots. Because these forms are being used on many of the public data sites, it is important that board members be comfortable interpreting them and using them to inform their decisions.

Use color to inform. A consistent use of color can provide instant information for board members, staff members, and the public. The traffic light is a good example. Green always stands for go; yellow, caution; and red, stop. We can use the same technique for student achievement. Green represents proficient; yellow, partially proficient; and red, not proficient. A similar pattern might be that red is below basic; yellow is basic; green is proficient, and blue is advanced. Depending on the number of performance levels being reported, more or fewer colors will be used, but red will always indicate high-risk or lowest performance, and green will always represent proficiency. Once colors are used consistently, colored graphs and charts allow for instant interpretation by anyone.

Use distribution models. Charts that simply show the number of students who met the standard or the percent of students who are proficient do not tell the whole story. Average scores also provide less information than boards require to make good decisions. Distribution models such as stacked columns, box-and-whisker plots, and scatter plots let board members know what proportion of students are at the various proficiency levels. They inform the board about the range of scores for the four quartiles of students and track growth performance in a value-added model. All of these pieces of information are needed for boards to understand the direction of student performance and the effects of targeted strategies and interventions. As boards join the accountability push for Adequate Yearly Progress (AYP) as defined in NCLB, being able to gather this evidence is critical to changing direction and improving student achievement.

Disaggregate all data. Many school districts have been disaggregating student data by gender and race or ethnicity for years. Others have not. NCLB requires accountability for four student subgroups: economically disadvantaged students, those with limited English proficiency, students with disabilities, and racial or ethnic minorities. Each subgroup must meet the standard along with the total population. School districts must monitor progress and provide interventions for each subgroup in order to meet AYP. To avoid cumbersome recalculation of data to meet NCLB requirements, all district data should be automatically disaggregated using the NCLB categories when the data is first collected and each time it is reported.

How Do We Manage Data Overload? How Do We Find Focus?

Use guiding questions. No matter how much data school districts and school board members receive and no matter what type of data it is, we can approach the analysis of the data by using a consistent set of guiding questions. There are three questions we always want to be able to answer, and all three start with the same phrase: How are we doing compared to … ? How are we doing compared to the standard? How are we doing compared to ourselves? How are we doing compared to others? These three questions represent multiple perspectives in viewing the same data. Each question plays its own role. All three perspectives are needed before boards and district leaders make changes or determine what is working and what is not.

How are we doing compared to the standard? Sometimes there is no standard against which we can compare a specific piece of data. More often than not, however, some standard does exist. That standard may be set at the state level, the district level, the school level, or even the classroom level. Comparing our data against the standard tells us how close we are to meeting established goals and gives us a measure of *proficiency*. Comparison to a standard is usually the first step in examining data, but it does not give us enough information to make good decisions and set directions for the future. The standards may be too easy or too hard or based on rules that do not apply to our population. At best, examining data on the basis of standards alone gives us an incomplete picture of the quality of the education our schools provide. At worst, it misleads us about our effectiveness. Standards are essential, but they are not enough.

How are we doing compared to ourselves? This is another way of asking, "What are our trends over time? Are we improving, declining, or flat-lining?" This is our measure of growth and improvement. Accountability models that do not consider growth and improvement will penalize those students and teachers who start behind and have far to go to reach the standard. Comparing our data to ourselves gives us our measure of *progress*. These measures have become critical to Adequate Yearly Progress (AYP), the accountability model in NCLB. We must always consider not only where we are compared to standards, but also where we have been. By examining our improvement trends, we can predict the likelihood of achieving our ultimate goal of proficiency.

How are we doing compared to others? This last comparison is sometimes frowned upon as raising too much competition in the drive for learning. Teachers are reluctant to have their students' results compared to those of other teachers for fear that teacher effectiveness and pay for performance will be driving forces in measuring educational quality. Teachers may also be reluctant to take on high-risk students for fear their performance will be compared to that of other students. Fairer models exist for making comparisons among students, schools, and districts, taking into account similarity of student populations, for example, as well as growth from similar starting points in student learning. These models are frequently called value-added models. The best reason to compare ourselves to others is the opportunity to learn from others and improve our own effectiveness. This type of comparison is at the heart of the continuous improvement organization. Comparison to others should never be for praise or punishment. Rather, comparison should be for the purpose of learning and improving our work.

Who should have access to the data? This is a complex question. We wish to be an open and transparent organization. As stewards of a public institution, we have an obligation to inform the public. At the same time, we deal with individual students and adults for whom we must protect confidentiality. That is why building a solid information foundation with a variety of accountability and reporting models is essential. As reporting and analysis tools become more sophisticated, we are developing models for analyzing our data that allow us to inform and monitor our decision making but protect the privacy of the individuals behind the models.

If a school district does not yet have access to these more sophisticated tools, district leaders must use good judgment and common sense in terms of who has access to what data. There is a delicate balance. The data should be analyzed to a sufficiently discrete level for the board and district leadership to determine specific actions for improvement. At the same time, public reporting cannot in any way allow for identifying the performance of individual teachers or students. School boards should not be using that level of information in any event. They should count on the professionals to examine the discrete data and bring appropriate group data together with trend information to help the board make the necessary policy decisions and set district initiatives.

Beyond the data required for public accountability, the school board should expect the development of an internal data-collection infrastructure. Such a structure raises the same questions about access.

Certainly, each teacher should have access to all data available for his or her assigned students. Traditionally most teachers kept their own records of student progress, which they may have shared with the principal but seldom with other teachers. As we move into a standards-based educational environment, schools are adopting a team approach in which teachers share strategies and student results in order to plan interventions and monitor progress toward mastery. Schools that have developed this collaborative approach to teaching and learning share their data openly as a basis for making informed decisions rather than to reward or punish students or teachers. These schools have already discovered the value of continuous improvement as a means to their desired end of improved student achievement.

The principal must have access to all student data in the school. The data must be made available in a timely manner, with the capacity to group student results by the accountability categories in NCLB as well as by teacher. Principals who are effective instructional leaders are "data junkies" when it comes to monitoring student progress. They verify for themselves whether students are mastering the required learning standards. They direct interventions for students who fall behind, and they monitor with their teachers the effects of various instructional strategies.

The school board has a tremendous responsibility to see that teachers, principals, and district leaders have timely access to well-defined data collected locally in a consistent and organized manner. The purpose of the data is to inform the ongoing decision making that directs the district's instructional program. The data is only as good as its capacity to predict readiness for the high-stakes assessments that will be conducted by the state in compliance with NCLB. We call such local data "leading indicators."

Leading indicators are even more important to board members than the final accountability results, which are *lagging indicators*. The goal may be to meet the state requirements and standards of NCLB, but by the time the board receives the accountability data, it is too late to do anything about it. All we can do when the final results come in is to try to determine after the fact what went right or wrong. The issue for school districts is to determine what is working and what is not working in time to change direction if needed. Using only the lagging indicators to determine a course of action is like playing the basketball game mentioned earlier with the scoreboard turned off until the end of the game.

Leading indicators are collected consistently throughout the year, not just at the end. Leading indicators are immediate feedback; lagging indicators are delayed. Leading indicators give specific information to determine specific direction; lagging indicators give only general direction. Leading indicators can be used to change results; lagging indicators cannot.

How Do We Determine the Effectiveness of Our Decisions?

School boards make hundreds of decisions yearly. Some are basic operational decisions. Others are policies and procedures that can change the direction of the district. It is critical that boards monitor the effectiveness of their decision making, especially at the policy and governance level. What evidence can be gathered, and where do we begin? Some school boards pass policies or establish initiatives without ever looking back. Future policies are introduced without reference to past successes or failures. Each policy develops in its own vacuum, and change is unrelated to seeking improvement. Other school boards attempt to determine the results of policies but are not always clear how to proceed.

Gathering the appropriate evidence is often quite difficult. Determining the success of an initiative or policy requires answering two fundamental questions. One of the questions is obvious: Did it work? That is really the second question. The less obvious (but necessary) first question is: Did we do what we said we would do?

Did we do what we said we would do? How do boards know that their policies are being fully implemented? Many simply assume that passing a policy makes it so. Others trust the word of the staff. The board has a responsibility to expect clear evidence that implementation has been carried out. This evidence should be provided not only for the district as a whole, but also for each individual school. The type of evidence that will be gathered should be determined and agreed on before the policy is implemented. That way, the expectations are clear up front, and the staff isn't being asked to provide confirming data after the fact.

It is not unusual to find that implementation is uneven from school to school. In fact, the larger the school district, the more opportunities for inequalities. While lack of full implementation needs to be addressed, it can also serve as a basis for data collection when determining the effectiveness of the initiative. When policies or initiatives are passed, we seldom hold out control groups because we believe in the action we are taking and want all students to benefit from it. By answering the question, "Did we do what we said we would do?" we not only correct false assumptions but also may provide a built-in comparison group.

Did it work? This second question can only be answered after the first has been resolved. And this question may be even more difficult to decide. The key to determining whether something worked depends on having clearly defined criteria for success. As Chapter 1 counseled, begin with the end in mind. What results did we anticipate when we passed the policy? What does success look like? How long do we expect it will take for the policy to have the intended impact? What evidence will we gather to determine success or lack thereof? Can we have partial success? What will we do if we don't achieve the desired results?

What About System Processes and Operations?

The discussion so far has focused on decisions that directly affect student results because improving student achievement is, ultimately, the key responsibility of school boards. That is not to imply that the continuous improvement process begins and ends at the classroom door. Business operations, systems processes, personnel practices, facility maintenance, transportation, food services, and all other support functions that make a school district work well can and should be viewed through the continuous improvement lens. Gathering data that reflects the effectiveness of decisions about system processes and operations is a key part of building an information foundation.

Ask yourselves the following process questions:
- How do we know that the processes we are using are as effective as we would like?
- What data can we gather?
- What input factors contribute to the success or lack of success in the final measure of student results?
- What factors do we control as a board?
- How do those factors correlate with the end results?
- What can we change?
- How will we monitor the impact of those changes?
- How do we spend our money?
- How do we allocate our staff?
- How do we invest in our human resources through staff development and training?
- What is our return on investment (ROI)?

School districts have a business side, and the board must try to make those business systems as cost effective and as service oriented as possible. Use the same guiding questions and approach to analysis that we have discussed in looking at student achievement. But the most important question to raise is: How do the various investments in the operations of the school system pay off for us in improving student achievement? Are our functions supporting our goals for improving student results? We should look to improve these facets of the school district and align them with our goals for student achievement. Our bottom line is still student achievement.

How Can School Boards Take the Lead in Shaping the Direction of Public School Accountability?

Keep it simple. Get started using the data you have available to you even if it is not everything you want it to be. Almost all districts, large or small, gather basic data, such as enrollment, attendance, graduation, and test scores. This is not new information in most cases, but how we use this information is changing significantly. Enrollment, for example, is no longer merely a count of the number of students. It also includes keeping track of the nature of the student clientele served by the school. Test scores have become not just a public report for school bragging rights, but rather a bottom-line accounting of school success or failure.

Don't be defensive. Understand that as more and more data becomes accessible, it is inevitable that there will be results and information you do not like. In fact, there may well be information you would really prefer not to know. The problems we don't know about are problems we can't be expected to solve. On the other hand, when we are aware of problems and the public knows about them as well, we are forced to act. Sometimes the actions we need to take are unpopular, but taking action is always preferable to ignoring or excusing negative information.

Don't blame the messenger. How board members react to negative information determines how much and what type of information they will receive in the future. No one welcomes bad news, so it is natural that board members are not happy when school and district results are not what they want. But if the board turns on the superintendent and staff, blaming them, demanding immediate answers, and expecting instant solutions, you can be sure that any future bad news will be obscured in some way. The board cannot generate the data; it depends on the staff to provide data that is complete and easy to understand. Unless this information exchange is conducted in an open and trusting environment, the organization will not be able to find the necessary solutions and meet the challenges before it. The board that receives data as a means to inform its decisions rather than as a basis for finding fault is a board on the road to becoming a continuous improvement organization.

Own your decisions. Too often boards let the superintendent and staff make decisions that are the responsibility of the board. The reasons for this can vary, but frequently the lack of good information is at the heart of the matter. In the absence of good information that is easily understood, board members rely on the judgment of the professionals. The staff's professional judgment may be very good, but the board needs evidence well beyond a sense of good will. It is important that board members seek facts and data to guide their decision making. The school board serves as a model for the entire district. Board decisions that are founded on open gathering and analysis of information reinforce that same practice by the staff.

The school board that embraces Information Age technology, together with a focus on using data as a tool to inform decision making rather than a tool for reward and punishment, is well on its way to building an effective information foundation. More importantly, the board members are creating an environment in which their information foundation will serve both their staff and their students as the driving force behind continuous improvement.

Scenario: Building the Information Foundation

Let's return to the scenario from Chapter 1 on closing the gaps among racial and ethnic groups' performance on SAT math. The board has examined the goal and determined that the goal is important and necessary to achieve. It now needs to look for different ways and new approaches to achieving its goal. Building an information foundation is an essential next step.

TAKING STOCK
First the board needs to take stock of the situation, answering the following questions:
- What data do we currently have about to the SAT math result?
- What do we already know about the problem?
- What specific test content analysis is available from ETS?
- What additional data do we need to gather?
- Do we have the capacity to gather that information?
- Do we have the capacity to disaggregate our data by race and ethnicity?
- What will it take for us to build that capacity?
- Do the people who need the data to make decisions have access to it?

TRENDS AND PATTERNS
Next the board needs to ask the administrative staff to look for trends and patterns through such questions as:
- What factors beyond race and ethnicity are predicative of performance?
- Which of those factors can we affect?
- Is our trend positive, negative, or flat-line?
- How do our trends compare to those in other districts?
- What other correlations can be seen?

DRILLING DOWN
To continue the information quest, the board must now begin to drill down. Suppose the board finds a correlation between the SAT score and the level of math course completed. The likely next questions would be:
- What determines how students are assigned to their math classes?
- How early in a student's career are these placements made?
- Who makes the placements?
- How can we intervene to accelerate students who have fallen behind the pace?

- How rigorous is our overall mathematics program?
- What level of preparation do our teachers have?
- Which students get the teachers with the best mathematics preparation?
- What other factors might be keeping our gap in place?
- What are other districts doing about this problem?

DECIDING WHAT TO DO

Depending on what it learns through the various drill downs, the board now needs to decide what to do. Board members ask guiding questions of the superintendent as they go through their decision-making process:

- What are we doing now that is working?
- What are successful districts doing to address this issue?
- What does the research tell us?

Any action taken must directly respond to the information gathered as a result of the drill down. For example, if the students who are falling behind in mathematics are assigned the teachers with the least mathematics preparation, the board would need to direct the superintendent to examine teacher assignment procedures. The superintendent, in turn, would be expected to bring back a plan for addressing teacher assignment and preparation. Such a plan may well challenge the board to review and revise its own policies in these areas. The revisions will require collaboration with the teacher organizations that may become confrontational. Nevertheless, the board is now making informed decisions, and the data gathered will form the basis of their decision.

MONITORING PROGRESS AND RESULTS

The final step in building the information foundation requires that the board monitor regularly the effects of their decisions.

Self-Assessment

Indicate the degree to which your board/district has achieved the following elements for building an information foundation.

	Fully Achieved	Mostly Achieved	Partially Achieved	Beginning to Achieve
We have all the data we need.	❑	❑	❑	❑
We receive our data in a timely manner.	❑	❑	❑	❑
The data we receive is in a format that is easy to understand and is disaggregated by student groups consistent with local, state, and federal requirements.	❑	❑	❑	❑
The data we receive is useful to us in our decision making.	❑	❑	❑	❑
We monitor and report data that is collected regularly within our own district.	❑	❑	❑	❑
We require our staff to use our internal measures as predictors of success on external measures.	❑	❑	❑	❑
We can determine the progress we are making toward local, federal, and state standards at the district, school, classroom, and student level.	❑	❑	❑	❑
We receive evidence that our policy, financial, and personnel decisions have been implemented.	❑	❑	❑	❑
We can connect our policy, financial, and personnel decisions through useful data.	❑	❑	❑	❑

We receive data that guides us in knowing
what is working, what is not, and for whom. ❑ ❑ ❑ ❑

Our annual report includes data on student
achievement and district performance
related to district goals and standards. ❑ ❑ ❑ ❑

The format of our report is consistent
from year to year and includes data from
prior years. ❑ ❑ ❑ ❑

We compare our data with other districts
that are similar to our district. ❑ ❑ ❑ ❑

We examine and discuss our data by
gender, race, and socioeconomic status to
measure the success of all students. ❑ ❑ ❑ ❑

We use our student achievement data to
make decisions and establish district
priorities. ❑ ❑ ❑ ❑

We communicate to the public how our
decisions are linked to student
achievement data. ❑ ❑ ❑ ❑

Principals and teachers use student
achievement data to make decisions
and set instructional priorities. ❑ ❑ ❑ ❑

We use our student achievement data
to plan staff development and to
recognize and reward teacher performance. ❑ ❑ ❑ ❑

We tie the evaluations of staff and of
ourselves as board members to the
data analysis. ❑ ❑ ❑ ❑

Use the self-assessment tool both to get started and to monitor your progress in
building an information foundation. Initial assessments may change as your
progress and understanding grow.

Questions for Boards to Ask

How do we use our data?
- How do we use data to make our decisions?
- How do we use data to monitor the results of our decisions?
- How do we ensure that the format in which we receive data is easy to understand?
- How do we use the data in our decision-making process?
- What data do we receive that measures student performance results?
- What data do we receive that measures our processes and programs?
- How do we use data to govern?

How do we manage our data?
- What would we do if we felt that the board is intimidated by data overload?
- Who defines what data the board receives?
- What control do we have over the data we need and receive?
- How do we ensure that we have sufficient internal data-collection mechanisms?
- How do we connect and relate our various data sources?
- How do we ensure that we have the technology infrastructure necessary to support our data-driven decision making?

Do we go beyond student results data?
- How do we use data to evaluate board decisions with regard to budget or action items?
- How do we share data with decision makers at all levels?
- How do we share data with stakeholders?
- How often do we monitor and review student progress, stakeholder perceptions, and program effectiveness by demographic subgroups?
- How do we ensure that we receive timely responses to questions we have regarding policy, personnel, and financial decisions?
- How do we ensure that our data infrastructure supports our need to analyze as well as report results?
- What percent of our monthly agenda focuses on reporting program results and targets?
- How do we use data to improve our system operations?
- How do we use data to determine which programs are the most effective for which students?

CHAPTER 3

CUSTOMER FOCUS

An essential element of continuous improvement is the concept of customer focus. Many educators and board members do not like to think of parents and students as customers. They argue that parents and students are not consumers who merely purchase learning as they might purchase a product in a store. Some educators prefer the term "client" to the term "customer," because clients receive a service and are active participants in the process. But whether we call them customers or clients, our parents and our students should be our focus in determining the direction of public education.

Board members and educators realize that students are not products of the public schools in some utilitarian sense. Students are individuals who bring an array of experiences, hopes, and expectations to the schoolhouse. The mission of the public schools is to enable each student to develop the knowledge, skills, and attitudes needed to become informed citizens and productive workers. Rich Harwood, a nationally recognized expert on reconnecting communities with the government institutions that serve them, points to the shortsightedness of viewing parents, students, and the community as consumers instead of as citizens who have both rights and responsibilities. There is something fundamentally wrong with the view of parents and students as consumers with no responsibilities for engagement in the process of making schools effective.

We have all been asked to complete satisfaction surveys by hotels, restaurants, hospitals, and car dealers. We understand why this information is being collected and usually appreciate the opportunity to give feedback about our experiences. How often are students surveyed about their satisfaction with the schools they attend and their educational experiences? How can we even think about improving a system without first seeing that system from the point of view of those it serves?

The Internal Customer

Let's begin our discussion of customer focus by looking at it from within the system.

W. Edwards Deming taught that having a customer focus requires constantly asking two questions and paying attention to the answers: Whom do I serve? Who serves me? In a system, everything is connected. The work of each individual affects the work of every other individual. Everyone in the system needs to know and understand how his or her work contributes to or impedes the work of others and how it contributes to achieving the mission and goals of the school system. So, for example, a school's sixth-grade teachers are customers of the fifth-grade teachers. In practical terms this means that the fifth-grade teachers have to understand (and perhaps negotiate) what the sixth-grade teachers expect students to know and be able to do as they enter sixth grade. Those expectations must feed into the planning of the fifth-grade instructional program. And on it goes, from grade to grade and subject to subject.

To use a district-level example, those responsible for procurement need to understand and use sound bookkeeping and accounting practices. They also need to understand how their operation affects the work of others. If school begins without the required textbooks in place, classroom instruction suffers. Those in procurement have to understand that impact and respond affirmatively. At the same time, the school staff needs to understand the time lines and challenges faced by those in procurement. Making this happen means establishing processes by which units and individuals within the system examine these relationships and define ways to help each other get the job done and done well. It requires intentional and transparent communication by everyone in a climate in which the truth is valued and problem solving is encouraged.

"Everyone" includes the school board. If the board does not focus on key issues facing the school system and delays politically sensitive decisions, the superintendent and staff are left in limbo. They cannot do their jobs because the board has not done its job. It is imperative that the board constantly seek to understand how what it does affects what staff does; that is, the ripple effect of its actions on the whole system. This means the board has to find ways to get feedback from those affected by its actions; in turn, staff members have to understand how their activities and the timing of their recommendations impact the board's work.

The External Customer

Now, let's think about "customer focus" from outside the system. Students and parents are those most directly served by public schools. Of course, individual citizens, communities, businesses, politicians, and university personnel are also affected by and have an important stake in the quality of public schools. A rich conversation that the board and superintendent might have in this regard is identifying the key stakeholders of the public schools in their community.

As the most immediate customers, students and parents know a good deal about their schools and how well the schools are meeting their needs. What students know is different from what parents know, but each group has a good deal of information and well-formed perceptions about what their schools do and do not do well. Many school systems conduct satisfaction surveys of parents periodically to gauge satisfaction, but these surveys are often very general in nature and do not probe specific challenges facing the district. Students seldom are asked for feedback by school leaders or school boards. Most educational planning and programming proceeds on the premise that others (the state, the school system, the school) know what students need and how best to provide for those needs. This mindset represents a version of the adage that children should be seen and not heard.

Continuous improvement begins from the premise that a school system (or individual school, for that matter) cannot make significant progress if it is not attuned to what its customers need, expect, and want from their schools. Feedback may come in many forms, but it is the lifeblood of any significant and sustained improvement effort. Margaret Wheatley maintains that "information forms and informs us" and the systems within which we work. Without information, it is almost impossible to know what is best to do. Instead, the tendency is to use past experience and success to make decisions about present and future challenges. The premise is that what worked in the past will work in the future and produce the desired result. The problem is that what worked in the past is confounded because the times and the circumstances have changed.

The World as It Is

Teaching methods that worked successfully 25 years ago may not work today because students come to school today with very different experiences and faced with very different expectations.

Today's young people were raised in a multimedia world in which information can be transmitted literally at the speed of light. They have learned to respond to several events at once. They do not have to shut the music off in order to concentrate on a book they are reading; they can play video games that require attention to the whole screen and call for instant and rapid responses with a skill that amazes their parents.

Contrast that world with the world most adults grew up in. In that world, sequential learning was stressed (reading from left to right, outlining and numbering to establish the logical relationship among ideas), and students were expected to study in quiet places with no distractions. Have you ever been frustrated by a video game in which more than one sequence of events was unfolding on the screen at the same time? By the time you adapted, the opportunity to act had passed. Even more frustrating, your children can play the same game with ease.

Students' perceptions and opinions are very different from ours. We must get information from them if we are to improve their learning experiences and academic performance. The same point can be made about parents and other stakeholders as well. Gathering input from our various stakeholders requires what the Key Work defines as community engagement.

Information as Lifeblood

Getting feedback can be done in a variety of ways, including focus groups, surveys, town meetings, board work sessions, and so forth. One caution, however—good survey instruments are not easy to design and benefit from expert advice. The same is true of facilitating focus groups. Staff members with such expertise and others outside the system should be tapped to ensure the instrument or the process is soundly constructed and properly administered.

In the remainder of this chapter, we will provide a self-assessment the board can use as a starting point, as well as tools the board and superintendent can use to promote better feedback and understanding of the needs, expectations, and wants of the key customers and stakeholders.

Self-Assessment

To what degree has your board/district achieved the following elements of customer focus?

	Fully Achieved	Mostly Achieved	Partially Achieved	Beginning to Achieve
We view students and parents as customers and clients.	❑	❑	❑	❑
We recognize and value the roles of students, staff, and other strategic partners in improving performance results.	❑	❑	❑	❑

We see ourselves as representing the school district as a whole rather than individual constituents.	❑	❑	❑	❑
We solicit feedback from parents, students, and the community at large on a regular basis.	❑	❑	❑	❑
We use this feedback to report successes and to measure improvement.	❑	❑	❑	❑
We collect and analyze satisfaction data by targeted subgroups.	❑	❑	❑	❑
We report to the community about the actions we have taken in response to important issues.	❑	❑	❑	❑
We analyze data from key stakeholders to determine patterns and trends that guide our decisions regarding budget, policy, programs, and personnel.	❑	❑	❑	❑
We compare our customers' satisfaction to that of comparable districts.	❑	❑	❑	❑
We compare our customers' satisfaction to similar data from the best-performing districts.	❑	❑	❑	❑
We have identified opportunities for improvement based on customer feedback.	❑	❑	❑	❑
We make decisions and set direction on budget, policy, programs, and personnel based on customer feedback.	❑	❑	❑	❑

Use the self-assessment tool both to get started and to monitor your progress. Initial assessments may change as your progress and understanding grow.

Questions for Boards to Ask

What do our customers say?
- Do we know who our customers are?
- What customers do we survey to determine satisfaction?
- How do we know how they feel about the value of the schools that serve them?
- How do we know if we have different levels of customer satisfaction?
- How do we know if any gaps in customer satisfaction correlate to identifiable subgroups?
- How do we determine if we have differences among racial groups? Among LEP, special education, or economically disadvantaged students and their parents? By gender?

How do we use customer input?
- How does the system collect, analyze, and use customer perception data?
- How do we use this information to plan for improvement?
- What processes are in place to deal with customer problems?
- How does the system gather information regarding the resolution of customer issues?

How do we keep the customer focus?
- How does the system regularly monitor improvement and make adjustments?
- How do we know if our improvement processes work?
- How is progress reported? To whom?
- How do we use this information to make budget, policy, program, and personnel decisions?

Reference

Wheatley, Margaret J. *Leadership and the New Science: Discovering Order in a Chaotic World.* (rev. and expanded ed.) Berret-Koehler and McGraw-Hill, 2000.

CHAPTER 4

CLIMATE AND CULTURE

Climate and culture are so interconnected that it is difficult to talk about one without talking about the other. Terry Deal and Lee Bolman describe culture in an organization as "the way we do things around here." It is a straightforward and useful way of thinking about culture. Those who study culture in complex organization add to the discussion many other aspects of culture, such as artifacts, stories that have achieved legendary status, heroes, traditions, ceremonies, and so forth. All of these are important elements, but the purpose here is not to provide a detailed discussion of the manifestations of organizational culture. The purpose is to highlight the importance of culture to continuous improvement.

Defining culture as the "way we do things around here" has several implications for school districts' efforts to ensure continuous improvement. For one thing, it captures an essential truth about culture: Successful organizations have developed ways of operating and solving problems that have worked well for them. On the flip side is that their success often blinds them to changing circumstances. Their thinking can become entrenched and drive out other ways of thinking about and solving problems. If, for example, the school district has a track record of success, it is likely to have a very strong culture, reinforced by substantial achievements. In this instance, the culture may blind those in the system to better ways of meeting present challenges. It does not have to be that way, but it frequently is.

Conversely, school systems that do not have a track record of sustained success are likely to have a negative culture characterized by defeatism and defensiveness. Usually the blame for failure is attributed to others. It may be the students ("If only the community sent us better material to work with!"), the parents, the facilities, lack of leadership, and so forth. Such a culture is negative and strong at the same time. It does not have to be that way, but it frequently is.

There is another scenario. School systems that practice continuous improvement successfully have built a culture in which the emphasis is on fixing problems, not on fixing blame. These systems make rigorous use of data to make decisions, focusing not on *who* is right, but on *what* is right. They reward individual initiative and celebrate individual and system achievements. The system seeks opportunities for improvement and ways to capitalize on its strengths. The impulse to practice continuous improvement leads to high-quality processes and high student achievement. It can be this way; too frequently, it is not.

Climate as Culture

Climate is both the byproduct and the bellwether of culture. Climate is manifested in the norms and expectations, usually taken for granted, that powerfully influence behavior. Students cannot perform effectively if the conditions in school are such that they do not know when someone will bully them, take their lunch money, or hold them up to ridicule. Teachers cannot teach effectively when students frequently misbehave, challenge their authority, disrupt classroom activities, and refuse reasonable direction. The climate in such a school impedes student progress and teacher effectiveness. Improving or changing that climate begins with serious examination of the culture that drives it. That culture may be specific to a school, or it may be the manifestation of attitudes prevalent in the district or the community itself.

So, what to make of all this? School boards that are serious about focusing on enhancing student achievement and fostering continuous improvement to achieve this end, must understand the culture of the school system and its major manifestation, climate.

Core Values

A good place to begin is by examining the core values of the district. What are they now? How do you know? Knowing is complicated because the values that are frequently talked about and posted for all to see are not necessarily the values that are really operating. Many school systems include in their mission and vision statements the belief that all children can learn and achieve at high levels. In reality, many of those same school systems also operate on what we call the "yeah, but" factor. The "yeah" is that all children can achieve at high levels; the "but" is that, of course, there are exceptions. Because of these exceptions, grouping and program practices have been put it place that reflect a different value, one in which students are rigidly categorized, grouped, and leveled according to the school system's expectations for them. In this example, the value that is voiced and the value that is actually practiced are quite different.

Whether you use the term "core values" or "guiding principles," the point is the same. One framework for continuous improvement, the Baldrige criteria, begins with core values that include *learner-centered education, creating or adding value*, and *focusing on results*. Think about these three for a moment. Suppose your school system is committed to these three core values: What has to change as a result?

How does a school system demonstrate that it is learner-centered? How should schools be organized? How about classrooms? The district office? Suppose as a board you are dedicated to the proposition that your decisions will be measured by the extent to which they create or add value. How will you use your time? These are serious questions, and they do not have simple answers. Boards and school systems that practice continuous improvement must begin by identifying and committing to a set of core values.

Being deliberate about the school system's core values is important. It is part of what we mean by beginning with the end in mind. Peter Senge once described values in an organization as the things we will and will not do to achieve our purposes and the way we expect to treat others and be treated along the way.

Good to Great

In the highly acclaimed book *Good to Great* (2001), Jim Collins and his colleagues examine the process by which successful organizations transform themselves from being merely good to being leaders in their fields. *Good to Great* challenges many of the assumptions we have made about leadership and key factors in the transformation process. It also examines issues of climate and culture as key ingredients in that process.

Good to Great draws attention to what Collins calls a culture of discipline. The significance of this culture is that discipline is internal and self-directed rather than externally imposed. The need for hierarchy and bureaucracy, so often a part of the culture of large organizations, is reduced or eliminated when individuals within the organization feel a sense of responsibility and self-direction toward the goals and mission of the whole group. Rules and procedures become less important than problem solving and results.

Too often, discussions of climate (and culture) focus on self rather than self-discipline. The perspective of the individual becomes the basis for determining whether a particular climate is positive. A positive climate often is described as one in which individuals feel happy, connected, and appreciated. The individual's perspective is an important one, but it is not the only one. In fact, school systems can have very happy employees with reasonably positive attitudes but still not be high achieving. The climate may be great from the employees' perspective, but something major is lacking if it is unproductive from the students' perspective. Employee satisfaction in and of itself does not guarantee a productive learning environment.

The salient question for any board that is pursuing continuous improvement is: How can we create a culture of team discipline—one in which programs and individuals are accountable for meeting or exceeding a defined standard of proficiency? Such a culture is described in the following terms in *Good to Great*:

- Freedom and responsibility are emphasized.
- People are in place who are willing to go to the extra mile to fulfill their responsibilities.
- Discipline is internal to the group and is never confused with a "tyrannical disciplinarian."
- All efforts and energies are organized to be the best at something (that is, to be the best school system at doing something).
- The truth, whatever it is, is always heard.

Picture a school system in which there are no clearly defined core values and the mission is assumed rather than clearly articulated. In this setting, dozens of random acts of improvement might well be underway, with individual schools and district office units doing what is in their own best interests. In this school system, the operating assumption is that doing good things will produce good results. In reality, however, lack of alignment produces competing and sometimes conflicting programs and initiatives. Taken together, these random acts of improvement absorb system resources and waste human effort. Despite evidence to the contrary, neither the board nor the staff is willing to abandon sacred cows, even when their care and feeding produce little in the way of tangible results. The truth, in this system, is often muffled and ignored.

Leading from Truth

The last point—that the truth is always heard—is essential, for it creates the climate that makes a culture of discipline possible. A climate of truth requires five essential practices:

1. Leading with questions, not answers
2. Engaging in dialogue and debate, not coercion
3. Conducting autopsies without blame
4. Developing "red flag" mechanisms that turn data into information that cannot be ignored
5. Creating a "stop doing" list.

What does it mean to lead with questions, not answers? Among other things, it means being open to new information rather than imposing tried-and-true solutions. Truth thrives on dialogue in which everyone has a chance to debate and be heard when important decisions must be made. It requires establishing mechanisms that ensure that the truth is not filtered and its implications neutered before it reaches those who must make decisions. (How many times are the board and the superintendent the last ones to hear about a problem that has major implications for the present and the future?) Finally, a climate of truth means being willing to stop doing things that are not working or achieving the purposes for which they were created. Understanding the culture of the school system is an important first step on the road to continuous improvement.

Getting a handle on the key aspects of the present culture will enable the board, working with the superintendent, to begin to challenge and transform aspects of that culture that are not helpful and that impede progress. It will move the board and the system toward a culture of discipline, without which any sustained effort at continuous improvement will fail.

Scenario: Climate and Culture

Let us turn again to the scenario that began in Chapter 1 and continued in Chapter 2. In this scenario, the central issue is the achievement gap between minority and majority students on the mathematics portion of the SAT. In Chapter 2, the board, working with staff, engaged in an intensive analysis of factors contributing to the achievement gap and devised several strategies for addressing identified issues based on analysis of the available data.

With renewed awareness of the key role played by climate and culture, the board turns its attention to the attitudes and assumptions that may be driving staff and student behavior with respect to minority student achievement. The board begins by revisiting the district's core values, and practices leading by asking questions: Have we identified core values? How do those values connect with the district's student achievement goals? How do we manifest these values in what we say and do? Have we affirmed these values in our communications with staff, students, and parents? How have we done so? Are there discrepancies between what we say we value and decisions we make?

In order to get a better understanding of attitudes and beliefs, the board authorizes the superintendent to conduct several focus groups among staff, students, and parents. The results of the focus group research points to several discrepancies between the attitudes and beliefs of key stakeholders and the core values of the district. Many minority students and parents express frustration about the low expectations that teachers have for them and the lower-level courses into which many are placed. Similarly, teachers report frustration with what they believe are unrealistic goals for many students—majority and minority—and the pressure to dumb down course content so that everyone can pass. Several other interesting findings are also discussed, among them the almost universal perception that the district schools rank well above average and that most teachers are competent and hardworking.

The board members realize that a major challenge in eliminating the achievement gap on SAT math scores is to change underlying attitudes about the ability of minority students to compete well academically. They realize as well that exhortation alone will not be successful. The board asks the superintendent and his staff to engage key stakeholders in an initiative that will facilitate an honest and open dialogue among students, staffs, and parents and lead to a broad-based affirmative action plan for the district. At the same time, the board decides to revisit the district's core values and mission to ensure that they reflect the district's commitment to providing a level playing field for all children, so that each can prosper and become a strong lifelong learner.

Self-Assessment

To what degree has your board/district achieved the following elements for climate and culture?

	Fully Achieved	Mostly Achieved	Partially Achieved	Beginning to Achieve
We share a defined set of core values that reflect the expectations of our community for high-quality public education.	❏	❏	❏	❏
We establish and communicate norms and expectations that inspire and motivate the district as a whole.	❏	❏	❏	❏
We recognize and value the roles of students, staff, and strategic partners in improving performance results.	❏	❏	❏	❏
We model what we expect from staff and others.	❏	❏	❏	❏
Board members treat each other with respect.	❏	❏	❏	❏
Board members treat the staff with respect.	❏	❏	❏	❏
We use tools and strategies that promote effective meetings and collaborative decision making.	❏	❏	❏	❏
We have processes in place for collecting, analyzing, and using parent, student, staff, and community input.	❏	❏	❏	❏
We have processes in place for incorporating stakeholders' needs and expectations to guide our actions for improving student achievement.	❏	❏	❏	❏

Use the self-assessment tool both to get started and to monitor your progress. Initial assessments may change as your progress and understanding grow.

Questions for Boards to Ask

What are our core values?
- How would we describe the culture of our school system to an outsider?
- What are our core values? How do we know?
- Who determines the culture of our district?
- What evidence do we have that the school board, administrators, and staff model mutual respect, professional behavior, and a commitment to continuous learning?

How do we deal with problems?
- How effective are we as problem solvers rather than problem presenters?
- How do we encourage debate and discussion of critical issues by our staff and our community?
- How do we use this input to guide our decision making?
- How do we promote problem solving that is data-driven?

Are we making the right decisions for our students?
- How do we determine whether our individual schools provide a safe and positive learning environment for all children?
- How do we ensure that student achievement is a regular part of our board agenda?
- How do we determine whether our decisions have made a difference for improving student achievement?
- How do we verify that our decisions have been implemented? How do we know that we did what we said we would do?
- How do we determine what worked and what didn't?
- What do we do when something doesn't work?
- What processes can we implement that will help us continue to improve our climate and culture?

References

Collins, Jim. *Good to Great: Why Some Companies Make the Leap—and Others Don't.* HarperBusiness, 2001.

Bolman, Lee G. and Terrence E. Deal. *Reframing Organizations: Artistry, Choice, and Leadership.* (3rd ed.) Jossey-Bass, 2003, p. 268. The quote is attributed to Marvin Bower, *The Will to Manage,* 1966.

Senge, Peter M., and others. *The Fifth Discipline Fieldbook: Strategies and Tools for Building a Learning Organization.* Doubleday/Currency, 1994, p. 41.

CHAPTER 5

PRACTICING CONTINUOUS IMPROVEMENT AS A BOARD

A great place to begin the continuous improvement journey is in the boardroom as a signal that the board is serious about continuous improvement. Board members cannot stand on the sidewalk watching the continuous improvement parade pass them by. The board must lead the parade.

We all know that what we do speaks more loudly than what we say. Most of us are familiar with the principle in organization development that leaders should not just "talk the talk but walk the walk." But do we understand the efforts required to make such a transition? Talking the talk is the easy part. First we become familiar with the basic concepts and tools available through continuous improvement. Then we must get our feet wet—we try the tools. Next, we reflect on what happened. What did we learn? How did it help us do our work better? Then, and only then, can we develop our skill level to the point that we internalize continuous improvement as the way we do business. Only then will we walk the walk.

A key concept in systems thinking is the concept of leverage. Leverage is the ability to influence what will happen. Everyone in an organization has some type of leverage—the amount of leverage depends on one's position within the organization as well as the nature of the decision to be made. For example, a teacher has great leverage within the classroom but less leverage school-wide. We all know of schools where the climate is chaotic or undisciplined and unstructured; even so, some teachers still set high expectations for behavior and productivity within their own classrooms, exert significant control and influence, and realize the desired results. Those same teachers, however, are at a loss to exercise similar influence over the school as a whole unless other staff members share a common culture and set of expectations. The principal, on the other hand, can exert great leverage on the climate of the whole school but has significantly less leverage over content delivery by a particular teacher.

As the governing body, the board has high leverage in terms of policy direction and district expectations. In other areas, such as how individual principals manage their schools or how teachers manage their classes, the board has relatively little leverage. The board can set expectations for what should happen in schools and classrooms, but its leverage comes in asking the right questions about the implementation of those expectations. Board members cannot and should not personally monitor schools and classrooms. This is the job of the superintendent and designated staff. But the board still has to know whether its policies are carried out.

Boards exert maximum leverage when they ask the right questions: How do we know that our decisions were implemented? Did we do what we said we would do? What is our evidence? Was the decision a good one? Did it work? How do we know? If it didn't work, what will we change? Such boards ask the questions, gather the evidence, study the data, and respond appropriately. The board that understands the concept of leverage is a board that understands why micromanagement is a dead-end street. When boards micromanage, Stephen Covey says, they end up in the thick of thin things.

Beginning with the board is not the only place from which to start continuous improvement. The superintendent and staff may already be using continuous improvement tools and strategies in significant areas of the system. If that is the case, the board needs to catch up and step out at the same time. But whether it begins or joins in, ultimately the board must be prepared to lead.

Opportunities for Improvement

Either way, a first focus for continuous improvement is the board itself. It is important to think of continuous improvement not so much in terms of what the board is doing wrong, but in terms of opportunities for improvement. This may seem a minor distinction, but in fact, it is the foundation for developing a continuous improvement culture. Continuous improvement is the difference between finding fault and seeking improvement. As individual human beings, we are constantly adapting to changing circumstances, not always because we want to but because we have to in order to survive and thrive. In the process, we learn new skills, abandon old ways of thinking, change attitudes, and begin to see the world differently.

Organizations need to do the same thing, but they are often less adept at doing so. Change is more difficult for larger and more complex systems. Consider the difference between making a U-turn on a jet ski and making the same turn on an aircraft carrier. The larger and more complex the craft, the more planning, coordination, and time involved to make the turn. Determined leadership is required for organizations to adapt effectively to changing circumstances. School systems that learn how to adapt and improve, thrive; those that do not, languish.

Continuous improvement, practiced deliberately and consistently, gives the board leverage to "grow" the school system's capacity to achieve its mission and goals. The first step is for the board to grow its own capacity to govern effectively. This means seeking out opportunities for improvement (OFIs) based on careful analysis and appropriate feedback. The board must be willing to put its own operations under the microscope to determine what it does well, its strengths, and what it does less well, its opportunities for improvement. For example, the board might find out that it makes good use of parliamentary procedures but does not come across to the public as responsive to community concerns. The former is a strength. The latter becomes an opportunity for improvement. Since OFIs must always be action based, the board might decide to change its approach to public comment at board meetings to permit more two-way communication.

It is not enough, however, to simply make a change in the procedure for hearing community concerns. At some point, the board will need to find out whether that change is having a positive effect on community perceptions about the board's responsiveness and whether other modifications in the procedure are warranted. The board will need some mechanism for surveying community members about how well the change is working. Without such a feedback loop, the board simply will not know whether it is achieving its objective. Indeed, one essential element of continuous improvement is regular feedback. Another essential element, implicit in this example, is that the board must do something in response to the feedback and be publicly clear about the action taken and why.

A Habit of Mind

Practicing continuous improvement as a board will take time, commitment, and persistence. In an earlier chapter, we spoke about continuous improvement as a habit of mind; that is, as a way of thinking about the work we do. It means being willing to be reflective about the board's role and about how well it accomplishes its work. It means being willing as an individual board member to be reflective about one's own role and contributions. The dictionary definition of reflection is "to bend back." Continuous improvement requires considerable "bending back" in order to understand what we are doing now and what we need to be doing in the future.

A good way to get started is to hold a board retreat to think through or affirm the board's mission and goals. It may seem redundant to some to talk about the board's mission and goals when the district already has a defined mission and goals, but it is not. The board needs to define its own mission and the things that it wishes to accomplish as the district's governance body. Next, the board needs to decide what the measures of its success will be and how evidence will be gathered. Finally, the board needs to develop ground rules for itself that are consistent with its mission, goals, and core values.

Another useful tool is regular, public work sessions during which a single major issue is examined. Such sessions need to encourage the free flow of information and differing perceptions. The work session is a perfect venue for inviting experts to address the board. It is also a perfect venue for engaging the community in dialogue. Productive work sessions can lay the groundwork for major decisions facing the board and the school system. Boards that use work sessions effectively establish ground rules that apply to the public and to the board.

Whenever the board thinks about continuous improvement, the term "feedback loop" should appear in the next frame. Continuous improvement is always data-driven. To practice continuous improvement, the board should be asking such questions as: What do we want to accomplish? What actions will be taken? How will we know that we have done what we said we would do? How will we know whether what we did made a difference? What kind of difference did it make? How will we know when we have achieved our objectives? What is the measure of success?

Scenario: Getting Started as a Board

To introduce a new scenario, let us suppose that the board has taken the important step of resolving to practice continuous improvement. The question then becomes where to begin. In this instance, the board schedules a series of public work sessions at which it proposes to accomplish three things:

1. Develop a mission and goals for the board for the coming year.
2. Adopt a board member ethics policy.
3. Establish a board handbook for the conduct of business.

Individual members of the board take responsibility for preparing background materials and facilitating scheduled work sessions. The board decides in favor of public work sessions rather than a series of retreats to allay any suspicion that the board is acting in secret and to open the process to public view and input.

At the end of each work session, the board conducts a plus/delta analysis of its work. That is, the board first identifies what was successful (pluses) about the work session; next, the board identifies changes (deltas) it can make to improve the upcoming sessions. Board members take turns leading the plus/delta discussion. Participants and observers are given opportunity for input as well. The results of each plus/delta review are summarized and reflected in planning for the next work session.

In its final work session, the board reviews and adopts its mission and goals, a board ethics policy, and an operational handbook. The documents are printed and made available to staff and the public in print and on the school system's website.

Self-Assessment

Indicate the degree to which your board/district has achieved the following elements of getting started as a board.

	Fully Achieved	Mostly Achieved	Partially Achieved	Beginning to Achieve
Our board has its own mission and goals that align with the district's core values.	❑	❑	❑	❑
We are familiar with the key concepts of continuous improvement.	❑	❑	❑	❑
We use the continuous improvement principles to guide our decisions	❑	❑	❑	❑
We have identified opportunities for improvement (OFI's) for the board.	❑	❑	❑	❑
We have identified strategies to address our OFI's.	❑	❑	❑	❑
We understand how to exert leverage to achieve our goals.	❑	❑	❑	❑
We avoid micromanagement.	❑	❑	❑	❑
We lead continuous improvement by example.	❑	❑	❑	❑
We understand the power of asking the right questions.	❑	❑	❑	❑
We have a feedback mechanism to determine the effectiveness of our decisions and actions.	❑	❑	❑	❑
We understand the challenge of change in a large, complex organization.	❑	❑	❑	❑

Use the self-assessment tool both to get started and to monitor your progress. Initial assessments may change as your progress and understanding grow.

Questions for Boards to Ask

- How have we defined the board's mission and goals?
- What are our strengths as a board?
- What are our opportunities for improvement?
- How do we identify our OFI's?
- How do we determine strategies for improvement?
- How do we communicate our OFI's to others and the strategies we will use to address the OFI's?
- What is our feedback mechanism for evaluating the quality of our decision making?
- Who do we ask for feedback?
- How do we respond to feedback we receive?
- How would we know when we're micromanaging?
- What do we do if we are micromanaging?
- How do we use leverage to achieve our goals?
- How do we empower others to use their leverage effectively?
- What continuous improvement tools do we use as a board?
- How do we assess whether we talk the talk or walk the walk?

References

Senge, Peter M. *The Fifth Discipline: The Art and Practice of the Learning Organization.* Doubleday/Currency, 1994.

Covey, Stephen R. *The Seven Habits of Highly Effective People: Restoring the Character Ethic.* Simon and Schuster, 1989.

CHAPTER 6

LEADING BY EXAMPLE

In earlier chapters of this book, we highlighted key elements of a sustained and successful continuous improvement program. Leadership from the board is critical to a sustained continuous improvement program. In the preceding chapter, we talked about ways that the board can turn the laser beam of continuous improvement on its own operation. When the board signals and demonstrates that it is willing to put itself under the microscope, seek feedback in a variety ways, and use that feedback to improve, it will send a powerful message to the rest of the school system. In effect, the board is leading by example.

There is a story told about Henry David Thoreau and Ralph Waldo Emerson. At the time, Thoreau was in jail charged with civil disobedience for refusing to comply with some law he considered odious. Emerson visited Thoreau in prison, and his first words were, "Henry, what are you doing in there?" To which Thoreau replied, "Ralph, what are you doing *out there*?" Of course, local boards are not being called to lead by example by going to jail or participating in acts of civil disobedience. Nevertheless, without the board's leadership of continuous improvement, efforts by the superintendent and staff are unlikely to be sustained.

Leading by example has many facets. One of these is practicing continuous improvement at the board level. Boards that create their own mission statements and goals aligned with system goals are practicing continuous improvement. In addition, a board that is serious about continuous improvement is constantly improving its knowledge and skills. Inviting experts and others to address them on important topics, holding work sessions that encourage the free flow of ideas, and scheduling regular retreats are ways in which the board shows its commitment.

Another way is to require a rigorous planning process at every level of the school system and to require accountability for results. The priorities of the board have to become the priorities of the system. Student achievement is the number one priority for all boards who are committed to the Key Work of School Boards, NSBA's framework for leadership. Keeping student achievement front and center, therefore, is leading by example.

Goals, Priorities, and Mission

Goals and priorities are two words that seem to go together, and for good reason. Goals are long range. Priorities, on the other hand, are more immediate and focused. For example, one of the board's goals may be to improve reading instruction because of poor student performance. The priority for the year may be to establish a staff development program in reading instruction for all elementary school teachers. That priority must also become a priority for the superintendent and staff. It is now up to them to plan and implement the staff development program.

In this example, the board's job doesn't end with setting the priority. Another role of the board is to allocate the resources needed to get the program up and running. The budget for the school district must reflect the board's priorities; otherwise, nothing much can be expected to happen. That may mean killing off a sacred cow or two to free up scarce resources. Still another role is to monitor progress, perhaps quarterly and at the end of the year. The resulting reports should provide data that help the board answer the two questions discussed in Chapter 2, Building the Information Foundation: Did we do what we said we would do? Did it work?

The answers to these questions must be informed by data in formats that give the board the big picture. Then the board must exercise its greatest responsibility. With information in hand, the board must make some key decisions: accelerate action on this priority, stay the course, make modifications, or pull the plug. The last alternative is a serious but important one. It is often difficult for boards to acknowledge the failure of an initiative, but when something is not working, we should stop doing it.

Another way that boards lead by example is to instill in others a sense of mission. Everyone in the district has an important role to play in the district's success. The bus driver's job is not just to get students to school on time, but to create an atmosphere on the bus that enables children to enter the school relaxed, confident, and ready to learn. That sense of "how I contribute to the work of the school system" is so important that, without it, very often the result is compliant but uncommitted workers who go along to get along.

Working through the superintendent, the board can ask each unit in the district to spend time thinking about the district's mission, goals, and priorities and identify ways that each unit and each member of that unit can contribute to achieving the goals and priorities of the school district. Developing and encouraging that sense of mission and providing opportunities for reflection and planning are crucial to continuous improvement.

Encouraging such conversations is the first step. The next step is to recognize individuals and units that are making improvements and contributing to the overall success of the school system. Celebrating successes at each board meeting will encourage others to become involved in improving the system's efficiency and effectiveness.

Aligning Resources

Leading by example also means aligning resources to reflect priorities. Consider the alignment required to implement a new program or initiative. The staff will need training and support to implement the new approaches and practices. It is not enough simply to bring teachers together for a half day to introduce the new program. When the change process is treated this way, systemic change is unlikely to occur.

Instead, the board must ask and get the answers to several questions. What professional development will teachers need? What time will teachers need for planning? What technology support will be needed? What support will teachers need during the initial implementation? Is the time line realistic? How will we know whether the new program is making a difference? Asking the right questions at the beginning will go a long way to ensuring successful implementation. Alignment around the desired end results is the responsibility of board leadership.

Determining what training, resources, and support will be required should be done cooperatively and in response to identified needs. The cookie-cutter approach to implementation almost always fails to accomplish much, because it does not respond to individual needs and concerns. It is simply not true that teachers and other staff members are automatically resistant to change, but they may resist being asked to change for no apparent reason. They are more likely to change when they see the need to change and have a voice in how the change will take place. It also helps when the time line is realistic and includes provisions for planning and practice.

Taking Risks

Leading by example means encouraging others to take risks and try new approaches. Not every attempt to improve will be successful. The board and superintendent need to create a climate in which experimentation is valued and it is all right to admit it when something does not work. We all learn from our mistakes, perhaps even more than from our successes.

That is as true of the board as it is of the staff. If staff members believe that the board is committed to trying new approaches and weighing the effect of those new approaches carefully and objectively, they are more likely to do so as well. Being open to experimentation makes it easier for the board to eliminate sacred cows, as staff members are likely to be less protective and more objective in their assessments of existing programs and services. When the focus is on *what* is right rather than *who* is right, change is evolutionary and continuous improvement flows from it.

Throughout this book, one of the transcendent themes is leadership. Indeed, that is the essence of continuous improvement. The board must be willing to face the most difficult issues confronting the district and not blink. The board must be willing to endure the static of competing interests and do the right thing. The board must be willing to make tough decisions even if doing so puts board members in political jeopardy. To the extent that the board ducks, others will duck as well. To the extent that the board stands tall, others will rise to the challenge.

Self-Assessment

Indicate the degree to which your board/district has achieved the following elements of leading by example.

	Fully Achieved	Mostly Achieved	Partially Achieved	Beginning to Achieve
We practice what we expect from others.	❑	❑	❑	❑
We are open to feedback from all constituents.	❑	❑	❑	❑
We respond constructively to criticism.	❑	❑	❑	❑
The district budget reflects our priorities.	❑	❑	❑	❑
We seek expert input as we deliberate issues.	❑	❑	❑	❑
We focus on what is right, not who is right.	❑	❑	❑	❑
We own the decisions we make.	❑	❑	❑	❑
We consciously align resources and actions to support priority initiatives.	❑	❑	❑	❑
We make politically unpopular decisions when needed.	❑	❑	❑	❑
We are first, last, and always advocates for our children.	❑	❑	❑	❑

Use the self-assessment tool both to get started and to monitor your progress. Initial assessments may change as your progress and understanding grow.

Questions for Boards to Ask

- What is the internal compass that guides our decisions?
- What are the core values on which we all agree?
- How do we ensure that we pay close attention to issues of alignment?
- How does our budget reflect our priorities?
- What was the last thing we decided to stop doing?
- How do we ensure that we are evenhanded in our response to competing interests?
- What politically difficult decision have we made during our term?
- When facing tough issues, do we move toward them or away from them?
- How do we know whether are we respected as a leadership group?
- How do we know whether our actions and directions are clear to others?
- How are children's needs factored into our decisions?
- What evidence do we have that we are courageous?
- What evidence do we have that we lead by example?

CASE STUDY

Building Capacity in Nashville, Tennessee

With streets named after such country music legends as Chet Atkins and Roy Acuff and with the enormous Opryland complex located just east of town, Nashville, Tennessee, calls itself the Country Music Capital of the World. This cosmopolitan city has a strong economy that is based not only on music and a $2-billion-a-year tourism industry, but also on health care, transportation, and automobile manufacturing.

Although the area's economy was thriving, the Metropolitan Nashville-Davidson County Public Schools (MNPS) had sung a different song for 30 years—a plaintive tune of low test scores, high dropout rates, deteriorating buildings, and a community that had lost faith in its schools and perceived them as mediocre. During much of that time, the district was involved in a contentious battle over desegregation. A 1971 court order compelling the school district to provide busing to equalize the racial makeup of its public schools prompted many white families to move out of Nashville or send their children to private schools. Finally, in 1998, a U.S. District Court judge released the district from court supervision over its desegregation plans, and the district developed a new, five-year school improvement plan that called for phasing out cross-town busing for students.

Nashville's school policy makers were ready to lead the district, which had seen student achievement stagnate for 10 years, into a new era. School Board Chair Pam Garrett recalls that education became the number one priority, as inspirational leadership, community commitment, and unprecedented levels of funding converged to change the culture of the Nashville schools. A visionary mayor and legislative council authorized $206 million to build new schools and refurbish others, to keep students in neighborhood schools as much as possible. Voters elected five new school board members who had a passion for education and realized its importance for the future life of the community. The school board hired a dynamic new superintendent and gave him the mandate to focus on achievement. Within a few years, the board's vision of creating a top-performing school district that emphasized success for each of its 70,000 students (55 percent are minority and 48 percent are eligible for free and reduced-price lunches) seemed attainable.

"We had an opportunity as a school system to be focused on children and achievement again, and that had not happened for a long time," Garrett says.

Continuous improvement became the district's theme, as the school board mobilized to meet the challenge of change in a large and complex organization. "Change is hard, as everyone knows, particularly in education. Education is a well-established bureaucracy in every city, and it's largely about adults protecting adults," Garrett adds. "If there's one thing we have done, and done well, in the last few years, it's been to focus the district and the community on what's good for children."

Nashville's efforts have centered on the school board's bold decision to adopt a new Policy Governance model, which incorporates:

- Procedures that help board members avoid micromanagement and concentrate on their roles as policy makers;
- A commitment to standards-based reform, curriculum alignment, assessment, and staff training, all based on solid data;
- A renewed and intense focus on respecting and serving the school district's students and parents; and
- Continuing efforts to forge close working relationships with the district's many partners in government, business, and the nonprofit sector.

Gathering and evaluating essential data were the important first steps in the change efforts. In 2001, the mayor agreed to fund a performance audit, conducted by an outside consulting firm, of every aspect of the school district's operation. School board members carefully studied the document, which provided an unbiased look at what worked and what could be eliminated, modified, or expanded, and authorized implementation of its recommendations. After the release of the report, which called for specific funding increases in many areas, the community passed the biggest tax increase in its history, with the money going to fund schools.

In July 2001, after an extensive search, the school board hired Pedro Garcia, a school leader with a reputation as a "no excuses" reformer, as director (Nashville's term for superintendent) of the Metro Nashville Schools. His mandate: to implement standards-based reforms and increase student achievement. A few months later, the school board adopted a vision statement and began work on a five-year strategic plan detailing goals, action steps to reach those goals, and an evaluation process. The board adopted the plan in March 2002, and Garcia spelled out his fast-track philosophy in a February 2003 report: "The community did not have the patience or the trust to see me hold hands, create task forces, conduct surveys, and spend a year or two determining what was needed to improve the system. We know what has to occur; we just have to do it, remain focused, and hold people accountable to do what is expected."

Governing More Effectively Through Policy Governance

For its part, board members recognized that, in order to be leaders and policy makers and to communicate the district's goals to the community, the board needed a governance model that avoided micromanagement. The choice was Policy Governance, which has earned a reputation for enabling governing boards to provide strategic leadership, to be accountable, to distinguish clearly between means and ends, to be involved in appropriate decisions without meddling or rubber stamping, and to set parameters for acceptable organization performance.

"We all felt like we wanted to govern a different way," says Garrett. "Board members have a real tendency to want to micromanage, but that's really not our job."

In the language of Policy Governance, the board's goals are expressed as "ends" statements, while the superintendent operates under "executive limitations," a term used to define the "means," or the ways things are done to accomplish the goals. The ends statements are not yet set in stone, because they are still under discussion, but they have already become the basis for fruitful, productive "community conversations" with such groups as the Chamber of Commerce Citizens Panel and the NAACP's Education Committee, Garrett says. The district's seven goals will continue to be discussed within school clusters and with groups of parents until the board winnows them down to five easy-to-remember statements. When the ends statements were omitted from a recent edition of the student handbook, the board insisted that a new front page be added, so that every stakeholder in the school system could be educated about the district's broad values.

The process will make it easier to evaluate the director, based on his progress in meeting the ends, or positive goals, and on his compliance with the executive limitations under which he operates. The school board has an annual agenda for monitoring compliance and reviews reports on different topics on a regular basis. In addition, says George Blue, the former school board chair, "We can call for monitoring at any point we choose by saying, 'Here is our concern, here is where you have not lived up to your end of the bargain.'"

Garrett likes the fact that the system will help the board focus on its priorities, clearly define roles and responsibilities, and monitor the school system's effectiveness. Garcia likes the fact that the system is geared toward results. "It is a helpful process. It measures what we should be measuring all along," he says. On the other hand, Garcia is being asked to take responsibility for areas he never addressed before. For example, an executive limitation in the facilities area calls for a process for interviewing and hiring an architect to make sure new schools are attractive and meet the needs of students. In the past, Garcia turned those issues over to a facilities director, but now he must validate that a process exists to make sure each new school meets the criteria. "Once we have done this [Policy Governance] for a few years, it becomes easier," he says. "At least that is what I am told."

For school board members, too, the process is taking some adjustment. For example, in the area of discipline, the administration had recommended establishing four alternative schools for students with chronic behavior problems. The board— sensitive to community concerns over the potential racial and economic make-up of the alternative schools—vetoed the administration's initial plan. Ideally, Garrett says, the board should simply have allocated the money to address discipline and evaluated the program a year later, but the board got heavily involved in the "how" of the issue. Looking back, Garrett admits, the discipline issue revealed that "we are still going through some of the birth pangs of getting Policy Governance right. We are still not there yet."

Improving the Quality of Reporting Results

Because the administration's strategic plan must match the board's ends policies and everything in the strategic plan has to be measurable, the school board has a serious interest not only in raw data but also in how results are reported. Garrett says she believes the administration has made progress but still must find better ways to report data.

The strategic plan includes 37 targets that the staff and school board are tracking to determine success and the action steps necessary to achieve those targets. To gather information, the district is monitoring results from a wide variety of assessments—including the state's Tennessee Comprehensive Assessment Program, scores from ACT and SAT tests, local data on student and teacher attendance and student discipline, data from Advanced Placement classes and examinations, and data concerning student involvement in activities and athletics. Principals are monitoring parent involvement and tracking the number of volunteer hours logged at their schools.

"If you want a board out of your business, hire an expert in every position, someone who can net out results and show the board, 'We are making progress,' or 'We are not making progress and here's what we are going to do about it,'" Garrett contends.

"We have great experts in place, but what we still don't have, in many cases, is the level of reporting we need to make decisions," she says. "We are getting there. With every monitoring, with every report, we are finding what it is we truly need to make a judgment on whether or not we are reaching our goals. That's been a painful process for both the board and the administration."

What the board wants is a single-page report on almost any topic—a report that would include trend data over at least the last four years and would recognize improvement and highlight positive results. An annual report would then provide substantially more detail on relevant topics. "Administrators by and large have a difficult time translating what they know for general public consumption," Garrett says. "Board members are lay educators; they are not there as experts. Part of our job is to be able to sell it [the school system] to the community. We need information in a form and format so that people can easily see, 'Oh, my gosh, we graduated 632 more students this year than last year.' ... It is important for the community to look at the [data] and say 'Wow,' and it keeps the board constantly armed with talking points."

As it compiles a packet of information to use in evaluating Garcia, the board is relying on extensive background material provided by administrators. "Everything they gave us is incredible background for board members who want to drill down into it," Garrett explains. "What we need is a picture on top of it. Show us in graph form, in chart form; show us how this year is different from the last three or four or five. Our number one question is: 'Are we making progress?'"

The board is willing to scrutinize its own actions and not simply those of the administration. At the end of each board meeting, members complete a Board Effectiveness Feedback form to help them examine how the meeting was conducted and whether they were prepared with adequate materials and information to use in decision making. This form surveys whether or not every board member studied the agenda before the meeting, participated equally in the meeting, listened attentively, and followed the agenda. The board uses the results as part of a debriefing that takes place in each session. Additionally, members of the board conduct an annual self-evaluation with representatives of the Tennessee Association of School Boards to assess their effectiveness.

Overall, Garrett says, she believes the board is moving into a posture that allows it to think about things before they happen and to become proactive rather than reactive. "During my first year on the board, as a system, all we did was stop the bleeding. There never seemed to be time to take a step back," she recalls. "Now we are trying to look ahead. I know what we will be monitoring next June; it's already on the agenda."

Building Capacity Academically, Logistically, and Physically

The Metro Nashville Schools are is emphasizing what Garrett calls building capacity in its academic programs, its physical plant, and its logistical support programs and systems. During his first year at his new post, Garcia led a dramatic and significant change effort in the academic area. He reorganized the central office and hired new personnel, including several administrators imported from his previous post in California; developed a standards-based K-12 curriculum aligned with state standards; implemented training programs for administrators and teachers; assigned principals to new posts; and gave special attention to improving literacy in the primary grades.

Curriculum became a major focus, with a wide number of board-approved changes implemented in elementary schools in the 2001-02 school year and in middle schools during 2002-03. For example, with 18,000 students in grades four through 12 reading below the 35th percentile, the district is strongly emphasizing training in strategies to teach reading. A K-4 literacy program is supported by $1 million worth of reading books and a reading specialist in every school. Reading is required for students in grades five and six, and older students who have fallen behind take a remedial reading class.

Other changes include piloting before- and after-school intervention programs that include bus transportation and materials for students, providing additional training for teachers of students who are English-language learners, and providing focused instruction every day on skills that students need to learn. The district also offered all 2003 summer school programs without charge to residents of Davidson County. Although students in the Metro Nashville Schools had the chance to enroll first, private school students who live in Davidson County were also permitted to attend free on a space-available basis. The board's decision to offer summer programs for the first time at no cost reflects its commitment to provide students with every opportunity for learning, school leaders say.

The district trained teachers in elementary and remedial reading, high school English, mathematics, and science. Some teachers learned how to teach gifted and special education students in the regular classroom, while others will use the knowledge to help students succeed in Advanced Placement classes. The schools are also forming vertical teams, groups of teachers in the same content areas in grades seven through 12 who will receive training in working together; the team structure should lead to more success in higher-level classes.

The Metro Nashville Schools are moving toward a standards-based educational system that is driven by internal assessments and not merely by state and national tests. These assessments, more varied and complex than the multiple-choice tests common to state assessments, will allow students to demonstrate their abilities to write and to solve mathematics and science problems and their knowledge of a broader curriculum. The district is piloting its own writing assessments at grade levels other than those tested by the state and will score these assessments systemwide on a common rubric so that different schools will not have different expectations. Since district leaders know that reading and writing skills develop together, their focus on writing as well as reading is an important part of their improvement efforts.

The district has also developed a brand new report card, Garrett says, which reflects the standards for each grade level. Every six weeks, every parent in the system will know what his or her child can or cannot do. The district is also concentrating on hiring new staff in the spring rather than in late summer, as well as implementing new standards for hiring certified teachers. At the start of the 2004-05 school year, the district had hired 1,200 new staff members and had only 30 vacancies to fill—real progress for a district that used to hire most of its staff in August. Now it starts hiring April 1.

The building of new schools and renovations to the physical plant are moving along well. Although, for the first time in four years, the school system had to make $22 million in budget cuts, it received $55 million in new monies for capital projects. Funds for building and renovations come from Nashville Mayor Bill Purcell—who, as a state legislator, authored Tennessee's educational improvement act—and from the Metropolitan Council. (Since 1964, a unified city-county government has governed Nashville and Davidson County.) "I cannot emphasize enough what a strong mayor and a strong council have been able to accomplish," says school board member Blue. "By outside estimates, we were $300 million behind in capital improvements. We had roofs that leaked in schools all over the city" before the metropolitan government approved the funds, he says. Three years ago, Garcia could not even plug in his computer, because he had no jack for his table modem, Garrett adds. This year, every teacher has a computer on his or her desk.

Four years ago, too, the school district could barely get a bus to school on time, Garrett reports, but the fleet was recently named one of the top 50 in the nation. The transportation situation was so bad that the board, inundated with complaints about misinformation and late buses, was ready to issue a cease-and-desist order. But the transportation employees came to the board, pledging improvement, Garrett says. "They practically formed their own corporation to figure out how to do better—and they made a compelling case to the board that they could handle bus maintenance, routing, scheduling, and every aspect of transportation." The board was very clear about its expectations, and the transportation department met them, she says. Now, she adds, transportation staff members understand how critical their role is to academic improvement—a message the board tries to convey to staff at every level and in every department.

Engaging the Community in Supporting the Schools

In addition to gaining support from the mayor and the metropolitan government, the school system has won the allegiance of a wide variety of community groups. For example, the Citizens Panel of the Nashville Chamber of Commerce examines all aspects of the school district and issues an annual report. Once Metro Schools receives the panel's report card, it asks each department to respond to findings relevant to its area of operation. In the group's 2002 report, Chairman Ted Helm praised the progress made by the schools.

"This past year has truly been an exciting one, to say the least, for our public school system and our community," he wrote. "It was a year marked by new and aggressive leadership; clear and dramatic mandates from our Board of Education;

bold promises; significant organizational, programmatic, and curricular changes; and the natural outgrowth of questions, unrest, and concerns that arise whenever an established institution is challenged with major transformation." For its part, the school board chair writes a letter to the Chamber of Commerce and other legislative and community officials, outlining what has occurred at board meetings and what actions have been taken.

Garcia says the Chamber of Commerce has a project that, through the United Way, aligns the school district's priorities with the funding requests of the non-profit organizations that want to assist schools. The alignment will result in a more efficient use of resources and will enhance the district's educational outcomes. "We have an opportunity to ask for help, but we want to be sure that what [organizations] provide aligns with what we need," Garcia says. He adds that individuals and community organizations understand that "we consider the school day to be sacred, and we don't allow community services to be delivered during the school day." Individuals and groups can tutor or mentor before and after school and during lunch, however.

The alignment efforts get everyone on the same page, supporting the district's strategic plan, Garrett adds. For example, there are 37,000 preschool students in the city, and every preschool organization now knows what the school system's preschool standards are and can prepare children to come to kindergarten ready to learn.

Last year, for the first time, the school board authorized a series of outreach activities to the public to gather feedback, communicate change, and answer questions. Staff members from the zoning, communications, learning support services, and magnet schools offices were available at eight different community information meetings, held throughout the county on Saturdays and during evening hours to accommodate the needs of working families. In addition, the board authorized the first-ever All Schools Fair, an event at a local mall at which more than 120 schools set up booths to showcase their strengths and programs. Approximately 5,000 people attended the event. Several board members who were present used the day to gauge public opinion on a variety of topics under consideration. The Mayor's First Day Festival, held the day before school opens each year, provides family fun, educational entertainment, and free school supplies and snacks.

The Metro Schools administration strongly believes that all stakeholders should have a voice. Toward that end, the superintendent is personally involved in establishing direct lines of communication with various sectors of the community. The superintendent's Parent Advisory Group and his Teachers Advisory Group have representatives from each grade tier (elementary, middle, and high) within each high school cluster. The participants meet monthly, bringing issues of concern to the table and serving as sounding boards for plans and activities.

To improve his relationships with the teacher and support staff unions, Garcia started an Anchor Group in September 2002. The group, comprised of senior cabinet members and senior staff from the three unions that represent the district's 10,000 employees, meets monthly to build positive relationships and to deal with issues of concern. An off-site retreat and dinner was held to discuss the parts each of the constituent groups could play in fulfilling the district's student achievement mission.

In addition, the strategic plan includes action steps to assess the trust of stakeholders through surveys of parents, teachers, and community members. It also calls for a professional review of the success and effectiveness of communications efforts. For the 2002-03 school year, the board authorized surveys of parents, staff members, and students that measured school safety, job safety, diversity, customer satisfaction, job satisfaction, and new teacher retention. Information from these surveys will be used to assess results, plan programs, and make budgeting decisions.

The board demonstrated its responsiveness to community needs when members realized that a large number of Davidson County residents could not read well enough to understand much of the information about school options for 2003-04. To remedy the situation, board members authorized the Communications Office staff to work with a nonprofit organization specializing in adult literacy to prepare materials, applications, and publications that could be understood by the majority of residents.

Learning to Serve the Customer Better

A few years ago, the school system established an information line that operated at certain critical times of the year and was manned by 10 people answering questions of all kinds. Now the school board is preparing to take the next major step in serving the public by supporting the establishment of a customer satisfaction department, something Garrett believes has never been done in public education. Planning is underway, and Garrett anticipates that the board will fund such an effort in next year's budget. Having a centralized customer satisfaction department will help the board know how the district is responding to constituent complaints and concerns, who is responding, how timely the responses are, and what the satisfaction rate is—information the board cannot easily track now, since four or five departments currently handle such calls. Garrett hopes that whoever runs the department will have extensive experience with customers. For example, a person who has worked behind the customer service desk at Wal-Mart or another major retail company for six months will know how to respond to questions and complaints.

"If administrators really wanted to do a service for their board, and get the board off their backs, they would find a way to effectively deal with consumer complaints," she says, adding that education in general has been in a defensive mode for too long. "People want to take things personally, but it's not about them personally," she contends. "It's about a system and a bureaucracy that sometimes is very unmanageable and extremely unfriendly to parents. ... Sometimes I think we look for reasons to say 'no' to people instead of examining how we can say 'yes.'"

Imparting a Passion for Student Achievement

The goal of the board and the superintendent for the Metro Nashville Schools is to create a school system in which change is welcomed and constant improvement is part of the culture. Garcia believes the system has tremendous potential. "We have many outstanding teachers and many effective principals," he says. "We have a large number of employees who are committed to making a difference in the lives of children. Our job is to create a system that supports them, validates them, and provides for them the training and the materials necessary to do the job effectively."

Garcia also wants to ensure that Nashville's ability to continuously improve will not depend on his or another leader's personality, but on a culture of change that becomes institutionalized. That will take time, but he is prepared to commit to the long haul. "We have made massive changes, but we still have a long way to go. Right now, we are a two on a scale of one to 10," he says. "This is at least a seven-year project."

The superintendent has advice for school boards and administrators who want their school districts to implement changes and continue to improve. "Assess where you are and face the brutal facts," he suggests. "It does not matter where you are, but where you want to go. Surround yourself with really good people. Stay focused on four areas—standards, staff development, curriculum alignment, and assessment."

Board Chair Garrett recommends that every school board learn to become an institution that functions at a high level of policy making, that sets the vision for the district, and that hires a superintendent who fulfills that mission. Boards should establish expectations and have experts who can meet those expectations and give the board a clear indication of results. "We are changing the system and the work of the board at the same time," she says. "It's hard work."

For more information:
LaVoneia Steele
Associate Director of Communications and Strategic Planning
Nashville-Davidson County Public Schools
2601 Bransford Ave.
Nashville, TN 37204
Telephone: (615) 259-8403
E-mail: lavoneia.steele@mnps.org
The district's website is www.mnps.org.

Signs of Success

The following results indicate the commitment of the Metropolitan Nashville-Davidson County Public Schools' to continuous improvement:

- Metropolitan Nashville students in 2001-02 made their greatest improvement in test scores since the Tennessee Comprehensive Assessment Program (TCAP) was first mandated in 1989-90.

- Across all subjects and grade levels, TCAP scores increased 3.3 percentile points (6.7 percent).

- Reading, language, and math scores in grades one through four (the district's primary focus in 2001-03) improved by about 10 percent (6 percentiles).

- In grades one through eight, 18 of the 24 reading, mathematics, and language scores were higher in 2002 than in 2001.

■ TCAP Writing Assessment scores in 2002 were 7.0 percent higher than in 2001 across the three grades tested (four, seven, and 11), with an overall increase of 41.1 percent since 1996.

■ An additional 1,164 Metro students surpassed the national average in reading in 2002, compared with 2001. Increases in the number of students scoring above the national average were even greater for language (1,584) and for math (1,932).

■ MNPS had 18 National Merit/National Achievement finalists and 23 semifinalists in 2002.

■ The district has set higher standards for its Scholars' Diploma, which recognizes outstanding academic ability.

■ Tennessee's 2003 Teacher of the Year was a teacher in the Metro Nashville Schools.

■ A student from Martin Luther King Jr. Magnet School won the state spelling bee for the third consecutive year, and a second MLK student won the county and state geography bee.

■ A Metro Schools ELL/Family Literacy Instructor received national recognition as the Toyota Family Literacy Teacher of the Year.

■ The Alliance for Public Education was formed and held its first formal meeting in February 2003. The primary focus of this diverse group of community leaders is to raise awareness of the needs of MNPS and to publicize the positive actions occurring in the schools. The group already has commitments of significant financial contributions, which will be used to enhance school services.

CASE STUDY

PLANNING AND ACCOUNTABILITY IN GAINESVILLE, GEORGIA

Located 50 miles northeast of Atlanta, the Gainesville City School System is the centerpiece of a thriving community in the foothills of the Blue Ridge Mountains and on the shores of Lake Sidney Lanier, named for the noted Georgian poet. With a diversified economy that includes a strong manufacturing base, a major poultry industry, and a growing service sector, Gainesville has withstood the economic downturn affecting much of the nation. Parks, lakes, walking trails, and a generally temperate climate have made the area attractive to businesses and the general public.

This little piece of paradise has attracted many immigrant and other workers who provide unskilled labor to the poultry processing industry. As a result, the Gainesville school system has a student population that is far more ethnically diverse (70-75 percent minority) and poorer (75 percent free or reduced-price lunch) than student populations in surrounding counties. District enrollment, which climbed steadily from 2,300 students in 1992-93 to 4,310 in 2002-03, is expected to nearly double by 2008. The number of Hispanic students, in particular, has exploded: 47 percent of students are Hispanic, and 24 percent are African American. Thirty-nine percent receive English-as-a-Second-Language services.

A fierce determination to help all children succeed permeates the district. Its five-member school board was determined to make the concept of No Child Left Behind a reality. "We felt that the system did well with a number of its students, and we were pleased with the quality of our products and services. But the achievement of minority and poor students was not what we wanted it to be," says School Board Chair Frank Harben. To meet the challenge, the school board committed itself to the critical concept of continuous improvement, which has led to many tangible results. Not only is academic achievement steadily improving, but the school board and superintendent are quietly spearheading a revolution in education—engaging the community, empowering teachers to succeed while holding them accountable, embracing innovation, and solving problems. Key factors in the district's success are:

- A carefully articulated common vision, mission, and core values, supported by measurable goals and objectives

- Strong board leadership, including a willingness to take risks and challenge existing practices
- The use of frequent pre- and post-tests to assess student achievement, a system to evaluate the superintendent's performance, and a variety of other data to guide the board's decisions
- A strong customer focus, which values students; gives autonomy, responsibility, and support to teachers; and seeks feedback from parents and community members
- A board that demonstrates a willingness to examine its own operations and looks for opportunities to improve.

When a long-time superintendent retired in 2001, the Gainesville school board conducted a national search and unanimously selected its new chief, Steven Ballowe, on the basis of carefully defined criteria. The board, searching for some-one who could think outside the box and bring in new initiatives, believed that Ballowe's excellent track record and deep commitment to students made him the right choice for Gainesville. "He had a history of reaching all kinds of kids at all levels, for innovation, and for creating wonderful learning environments for kids," Harben says. Ballowe expresses his philosophy this way: "Our mission is to make children's dreams a reality. The culture is completely focused on students. We exist for the children."

Articulating a Common Vision and Core Values

In conversations with its stakeholders, at its board meetings, in articles, and through its website, the Gainesville school board has articulated its common set of beliefs, mission, and goals, revisiting them when necessary. "We share a common mission and a common vision, and the superintendent shares it as well," Harben says. "Our community recognizes that public education is one of the pillars of a democracy. It's terribly important to have an educated population that knows and understands its rights and has the knowledge to protect those rights." Through its partnership with the superintendent, the board began to act on its beliefs that all students can learn and contribute, that higher expectations encourage higher per-formance, that a climate of healthy risk-taking encourages learning, that learning is a continuous and rewarding process, and that personal and organizational improvement require ongoing effort.

Together, Ballowe and the school board immediately began to make changes to improve the school system and to devise a strategic plan that would allow for improvement each year. This Performance Accountability Plan, established in 2001, makes all school employees accountable for fostering achievement for all students. The plan is disseminated widely, with copies made available to each school and to the public on the Internet. By communicating their goals and objectives to the community, school leaders not only make it clear which goals and objectives are important to accomplish during the school year, but they also invite parents and community members to become part of the change, Ballowe says. The plan, he adds, eliminates bickering or disagreements over roles and responsibilities and allows elected school officials to make an impact on the direction in which the school district is moving.

The Performance Accountability Plan has five broad goals: to educate all children in Gainesville City to be successful students; to provide fiscal accountability to the citizens of the city and the county; to provide clean, safe, and educationally appropriate facilities conducive to learning; to provide an atmosphere for staff to become innovators and risk-takers; and to have continuing dialogue with the various communities involved with the school system. Each goal has numerous objectives, which are supported by action plans designed to achieve specific aspects of the broader goal. The superintendent and all administrators use quantifiable measures to assess how well each objective has been implemented.

"The Performance Accountability Plan takes the vision of the board, creates objectives, and quantifies to the extent possible what growth, success, and progress mean," explains Harben. "It was a collaborative process. We met with Dr. Ballowe during a retreat process and developed our vision and goals. Dr. Ballowe then came back with a list of objectives to satisfy the goals," adds Harben. "We wanted to make the goals quantifiable. If a goal were to improve fifth-grade reading, we needed to know by how much and when. Being able to measure progress takes the subjectivity out of the process and helps us understand what we did right and what we should do differently."

Exercising Strong Board Leadership

As a first step toward serving students better, the school board and superintendent created a system of "academies of excellence"—essentially restructuring the Gainesville school system by providing parents with choice. The board exercised its leadership role when it addressed community concerns that the choice plan might lead to a racially or economically segregated school district or that resources would be allocated inequitably among the academies. "There was a lot of trepidation, but the board showed courage because we really believed that the plan was in the best interests of children, and we wanted to deliver services based on that [idea] rather than on political expediency," Harben says. He adds that the board members presented a united front that "got us over the hump as we got the changes in place."

The district held dozens of public meetings—many in Spanish and some in Thai—to discuss options and opportunities. The key points were to be "creative and innovative," Ballowe explains. Providing school choice helped foster the climate of empowerment and accountability so important to board members and the superintendent, who contend that parents who have a choice take more responsibility for their children's achievement. At the same time, teachers and administrators also feel more accountable when they create from the bottom up, district leaders say. "We broke the mold of top-down decision making," says Ballowe. "When something comes top down, a person can say, 'That was a dumb idea.' But we challenged them to create from the ground up and to take ownership."

The process quickly led to the creation of five new academies—three located in existing elementary school buildings and two in new schools built to accommodate the growing school population. Each academy has a different focus—emphasizing science and math, fine arts, or providing an International Baccalaureate program, for example—but each features the state's core curriculum, special education services, technology laboratories, bilingual assistance, literacy coaches, after-school programs, and other important programs. Every academy has a site-based budget, and all schools have active Parent-Teacher Associations, school councils, and partners-in-education programs.

The district provides free busing to transport students to schools within their transportation zone; shuttle buses then take the children to their schools of choice. "We were able to create a centralized, efficient system that actually shortened many of the bus routes, and we don't have as many buses going to the same areas," Ballowe says. Best of all, all parents were able to send their children to the academy that was their first choice. Overall, the choice plan has generated much satisfaction, Harben says, noting that, for the 2004-05 academic year, more than 90 percent of students are staying at the school their families originally selected.

Because continuous improvement has become a habit of mind, the school board is already thinking ahead to fine-tune the elementary school choice process if necessary. For example, one school currently enrolls 700 students, while another—a new school that was still under construction when families were asked to make their choices—has only 350. Over time, student enrollments are expected to equalize, Harben says, but the board will be keeping an eye on demographic trends. "If we have a program that is not attracting people or performing as well [as others], we will look at that," he says. "And there will come a time when we will have to address space issues."

At the middle school level, Gainesville Middle School created three academies within its walls—emphasizing classical studies, humanities, and science and ecology. The academies were designed after an intense study by the faculty and administration, with input from parents and students. Students remain with the same teams of teachers for three years, a structure that creates a smaller school environment and fosters closer bonds between teachers and students. Noting that one size does not fit all, Harben says the middle school academies allow faculties to create their dream course of study while still providing solid core programs.

At the high school, changes are constantly being made to improve and expand the academic offerings, challenge students, and encourage them to graduate so they can fulfill their career aspirations. While administrators work hard to offer more Advanced Placement (AP) courses and to improve scores on the SATs, they also emphasize the expansion of the district's career education and technical programs. Surveys of seniors' post-graduation plans indicate that, while 62 percent expect to attend a four-year college, 17 percent plan to attend a two-year college and 16 percent a technical college.

Aware that many students work or have other obligations to their families, the school board and administrators are also providing more flexible scheduling. "At the high school, kids sometimes could not take a course they needed because of scheduling problems," Ballowe says. "But if a youngster needs something, we have to make it happen." The high school already offers a good deal of flexibility and choice. Some courses are part of a "4x4" block: Four classes meet full time during the first semester, and an entirely new set of classes is offered during the second semester. Other courses meet daily or every other day for a full year. During the 2004-05 academic year, the school is also offering early-morning and late-afternoon classes; teachers' contracts are being rewritten to allow some staff members to start and stop teaching later in the day. "Next year, if a student wants to attend school 11 a.m. to 6 p.m., so be it," he says.

Ultimately, Ballowe expects to have all schools open from 7 a.m. to 7 p.m. by partnering with community groups. "How do we make sure we have 7-7 schools? I throw out options and ideas and remove the obstacles," Ballowe says. "The school's job is to decide which options work best. But we can do it with the same money and the same number of staff."

Measuring Progress During the Year

With the basic academic structures in place, the board and superintendent are now striving to measure progress toward their goals using an annual time line. The board meets twice a month. One meeting is a work session at which the board collects information but takes no action. At its other monthly meeting, the board spends much of its time updating the Performance Accountability Plan using progress reports that also identify the procedures staff members are using to meet objectives. "We get a schedule at the beginning of the year, and we receive reports on a regular basis," says Harben. "We don't want to wait until the end of the year and then say, 'What happened?'"

Quarterly, the superintendent evaluates all administrators and updates the progress of implementation. In April, the superintendent documents the results for each objective. In May, the board evaluates each objective individually and creates a consensus score. Harben and the board's secretary compile a summary of the ratings and comments, and the board meets privately to discuss the document. During its June retreat in Savannah, the board meets with the superintendent to discuss his evaluation, which is based on his success in meeting the plan's objectives. The board and superintendent also identify ongoing or new objectives and assign critical weights, indicating which objectives are most important to the leadership. In July, the leadership team starts the process all over again, announcing the upcoming school year's objectives, and asking the superintendent and administrators to create action plans.

One example illuminates how the accountability process operates. An objective under Goal 1 (to educate all children to be successful students) is to increase the number of students passing Advanced Placement exams with a score of three (out of a possible five) by 3 percent over the previous year. During quarterly evaluation meetings and in presentations to the school board, Gainesville High School Principal David Shumake or his assistant principals discussed the steps taken to meet this objective.

To help improve scores, administrators and faculty devised an action plan that calls for communicating the expectations of AP courses to students, providing summer reading lists for AP history and all levels of English, covering all AP course material before the AP calculus test, providing increased writing opportunities with data-based questions for the U.S. history course before the examination, holding after-school review sessions, providing study guides and supplementary materials for AP biology students, and discussing strategies for AP exams. Although there had been gains in previous years, the percentage of students scoring three or better on the AP tests decreased from 56.1 percent in 2001-02 to 54 percent in 2002-03—a statistic the administration and school board will discuss so they can determine why the objective was not met.

When they review the superintendent's progress in meeting the objectives listed under each broad goal, board members use a scale of 1 ("needs improvement") to 5 ("outstanding"). Any score of 1 must have an explanation. The scores are compiled, and average, medium, and mode scores are calculated for each objective.

The board, however, uses a statistical "consensus" model, developed by Harben, which reflects the majority's views and prevents any one disgruntled board member from skewing the scores. "The superintendent's evaluation is not the sum and then the average of each individual board member's evaluation," he says. "The board as a group determines the evaluation." If, for example, three board members score progress on a particular objective a "5," one scores it a "4," and one scores it a "1," the average score would be four. But that score would not reflect the way the board as a whole would vote, Harben says.

Using Harben's model, the consensus score would be a "5." The consensus approach is a time-saving device that helps board members communicate with each other and prevents one individual from tainting the evaluation, he explains. The board as a whole always votes whether to accept the scores and determines whether the scores reflect the consensus of the board.

As part of the goal-setting process for 2002-03, the board further improved the evaluation system by determining which objectives are most important. The high priority items—such as improvements in reading and math scores—carry more weight in the superintendent's overall evaluation than other objectives ranked lower on a 1-5 scale. "The board tells me which objectives are really important and helps me maximize the expenditure of resources," Ballowe says.

The board also evaluates which objectives should remain from year to year, which should be modified or deleted, and which new objectives need to be added. For example, the board added 10 new objectives for 2003-04. One important new objective for Goal 1 (educating all children to be successful), given a weight of "4," is to create a K-12 technology curriculum that addresses all state requirements for the mastery of computer skills and to assess the levels of training and competency faculty and staff have achieved. An important objective for Goal 2 (provide fiscal accountability), weighted a "5," is to review all existing school and district financial procedures and provide recommendations for accountability by January 1, 2004. Although most objectives remain in force from year to year, some which are more time-limited—such as passing a local sales tax—are eliminated when the issue is resolved.

"Our Performance Accountability Plan is a living, breathing document," Ballowe explains.

One problem, however, is that much of the data used in the evaluation trails behind the school year. Data the district compiles in-house—such as absentee rates and referrals to alternative schools—reflect the school year just completed, but state and national test score data come too late for the board's June evaluation. As a result, the superintendent, of necessity, is rated on some measures for the school year that just ended and on other measures that reflect progress during the previous school year.

How well did the superintendent do in his first two years? In 2001-02, his overall consensus score was 4.16. For 2002-03, he earned an overall consensus score of 4.37—based on the newer system of weighted priority objectives. The superintendent's evaluation is published on the district's website, where it is made available to the public. "It takes a lot of courage on the part of Dr. Ballowe to be willing to be held accountable and to say, 'Here's where I did well, here's where I did not do so well,'" Harben says. "It's commendable."

Measuring Students' Progress

As it moves to the next stage of improvement, the school system plans to gather and publish more data and more documentation to help it assess progress. Currently, the district's evaluation emphasis is on pre- and post-testing on a nine-week cycle. Teachers first review state standards to determine what needs to be taught and when; the teachers then pretest students so they can construct lesson plans that determine how, as a group, they will teach the period's standards. Because the teachers have a good idea of what students know and don't know, they can focus more precisely on what they need to cover. Every nine weeks, teachers at all levels publish the results of the pre- and post-tests, with no names attached, outside their classrooms. To ensure that every teacher knows how to teach each standard, the district supplies literacy coaches to work with individual teachers on reading, writing, and mathematics and to give teachers strategies to improve performance. "This is not about being punitive, but about being supportive," Ballowe says. The district is also attempting to create a database of methods that can be used to successfully teach each objective. "We are a full-time standards-based system," he says.

The school board's role is to monitor progress, Harben says. "We have empowered teachers to develop their own styles and their own learning environments. That's properly a board role—to allow folks latitude and freedom rather than enforce a scripted method [of teaching]." As a result of the district's policies, which emphasize staff improvement, he adds, "we are seeing a lot more teaming and sharing of best practices."

Constant reinforcement and monitoring help ensure that the school system "walks the talk," notes Ballowe. "Too often, we have been too concerned with, 'Are the employees happy?' The real question is, 'Are the kids learning?' If it's what children need, let's make it happen."

The district also uses surveys to gauge its customers' views. For example, it surveyed parents, students, and teachers to see how many wanted school uniforms. Results indicated that the community wanted uniforms at the elementary school level, where they are now required, "modified uniforms" in middle school, but no uniforms in high school. District leaders also plan to survey their customers about the possibility of year-round schooling, to determine what options might best meet students' needs.

Because the school district has many Hispanic students, the school board and administrators have read research about cultural and educational norms in the Hispanic community. In certain situations, for example, Hispanic parents, who respect the authority of the school, might hesitate to question why a child was placed in a certain setting. To encourage more effective communication, the school board has become an advocate of home visits. Now, administrators go to the homes of new students, a practice that Harben says is socially acceptable and beneficial.

Board members also visit schools frequently, dropping by or scheduling lunch with administrators. "It's part of our leadership role and makes a statement. It shows students and teachers that we care about them," Harben explains.

To strengthen their common vision and shore up their core values, from time to time the school board members and all administrators and central staff read the same book and schedule a joint meeting to discuss the ideas and concepts conveyed in the book. They have already discussed *No Excuses,* by Abigail and Stephan Thernstrom, which sends a tough message about closing the racial gap in academic achievement. Now they are gearing up to discuss *Leading With the Heart: Strategies for Basketball, Business and Life,* by Mike Krzyzewski, Duke University's famed basketball coach. The book explains why compassionate, focused, and highly flexible leadership skills are necessary in all walks of life.

In the planning stage is a community reading program that would focus on one or two books a year. The books might be discussed at PTA meetings, in the library, or through articles featured in the local press. The object, Harben says, is to create a community dialogue: "There is a lot of dialogue that needs to happen to bring a community closer together."

Putting Its Own Operations under a Microscope

To do its job well, the school board must not only monitor how well administrators, teachers, and students are performing, but it must also evaluate its own performance. Is the board avoiding micromanagement? Is it identifying opportunities for improvement? Does it understand the challenge of change in a complex organization? Each year, at a retreat, the board undertakes a formal self-evaluation process to determine how well it is adhering to certain agreed-on protocols and to assess its relationship to the community, taxpayers, and the school system as a whole. For example, the board has a protocol to handle complaints from parents, a process that gives the appropriate person at each level—the teacher, the principal, or the superintendent—an opportunity to resolve issues.

As board chair, Harben acknowledges that he and the other board members often walk a tightrope when a parent calls them directly. As elected public officials, they want to be responsive to community concerns, but they also want to show respect for process. They often handle complaints by explaining the process but encouraging a parent to call back and tell the board member whether the issue has been resolved and whether the parent is satisfied with the result. "We don't want to be so rule-bound that we cannot address needs as they come along," he says.

More informally, board members have agreed to be accountable to one another. The board has created an environment in which it is permissible for a board member to tell Harben, for example, "You've stepped over the line here, Frank." Open communication, rapport, and mutual respect have made it possible for the school board to provide a high level of leadership. "Our board has a very high caliber of individuals," Harben says. "Every board member says, 'I'm not here just to represent the people who elected me, but to do what's best for every child and to improve every child's achievement.'"

Charting the Future

The board and superintendent recognize that, while many objectives are being met, the school system still has a considerable way to go to accomplish all of its goals. Already, however, the Performance Accountability Plan has had a profound effect on the school district's culture. "We no longer accept excuses for poor performance," says Harben. "We now have a culture of success that says all students can learn and achieve."

At the same time, Harben adds, the goal is not simply to achieve high test scores but to continually improve, to produce good citizens and well-rounded individuals, and to emphasize that learning is a life-time pursuit. "We want good test scores, but they are the by-products of other things we are doing right," he says.

The school board and superintendent have learned that sound and intelligent planning must be matched by an equally strong commitment to stay the course and to make mid-course corrections where necessary. Harben urges school boards and superintendents to "make a commitment to work together to the greatest extent possible in a professional and harmonious manner. Try to stay balanced and take a long-term view. And have realistic goals and expectations—that's the key."

For more information:
Steven E. Ballowe
Superintendent
Gainesville City School System
508 Oak Street, N.W.
Gainesville, GA 30501
Telephone: (770) 536-5375
E-mail: steven.ballowe@gcssk12.net
The district's website is http://www.gcssk12.net.

Signs of Success

The following results are indicators of the Gainesville City School System's commitment to continuous improvement:

- The community was heavily involved in creating and then choosing ideal teaching and learning environments. During the second year of the academies of excellence" program, 100 percent of parents received their first choice of academies for their children.

- The district is taking an active advocacy role with the state's General Assembly and the governor to promote a focus on nurturing students who have the skills to become outstanding citizens and contribute to the community. Great importance is placed on building school-community partnerships that expand the classroom from the brick and mortar of a campus building to the community. As a result, many positive outcomes, such as partners-in-education programs, are occurring.

- SAT participation by minority students has improved. The number of African-American students taking the SAT went from just two students in 2001-02 to 42 in 2002-03. The average SAT score rose from 990 in 2000-01 to 1012 in 2001-02.

- More students are taking Advanced Placement tests. During 2000-01, 82 tests were taken; during 2001-02, the number was 126 tests.

- The number of students taking Carnegie-level courses at Gainesville Middle School rose from 64 in 2001-02 to 181 in 2002-03.

- Individual teacher accountability has improved with the implementation of quarterly pre- and post-tests, which were piloted in the 2002-03 school year.

CASE STUDY

WORLD-CLASS RESULTS IN MILLARD, NEBRASKA

Millard, Nebraska—developed by Ezra Millard more than 125 years ago from an uninhabited prairie 12 miles southeast of Omaha—is now a vibrant suburb in the heartland of America. Millard Public Schools is one of the fastest-growing districts in the state. During the 1960s, a merger with seven rural districts fuelled explosive growth, and the district reached its present size of 35 square miles. Although later decades saw turbulent times, as attempts were made to annex the Millard schools into the Omaha Public Schools first in 1971 and again in the late 1980s, the school district remained independent and is now the third largest in the state.

Once concerns about merger and consolidation were laid to rest, the district's policy makers and administrators began to focus close attention on academic achievement. Through its strategic planning efforts, which began in 1990, the district has demonstrated steady academic progress. The district enrolls approximately 20,000 students, most of them white and middle class; only 5 percent receive free or reduced-price lunch. Ninety-four percent of seniors graduate from high school; 90 percent enroll in college and 90 percent of those students remain in college after freshman year. But being a very good district was not enough: Millard's school leaders were going for great.

In March 2004 the school board was confident enough to approve a bold new mission statement for the next five years: to *guarantee* that all students will be prepared for personal success and responsible citizenship in a global society by creating a world-class educational system characterized by innovative and diverse opportunities designed to challenge each student.

"We feel that Millard is an excellent school system, but we aspire to create a world-class educational system," says School Board President Jean Stothert. "We will guarantee—not hope, but guarantee—that all students learn the academic and life skills they need to succeed. We feel we can make this guarantee because of our assessment system and our curriculum. Now our first challenge is to determine what 'world class' means."

The school district's success in continuous improvement stems from several important factors:

- A mission and strategic plan, accompanied by action plans, that are re-evaluated every five years and developed with community support
- Bold school board leadership, including a willingness to address controversial political issues, such as raising taxes
- The ability to recognize and value the roles of students, parents, staff members, and community partners in improving performance
- An educational program that uses clearly defined and measurable standards to ensure that all students learn the requisite skills
- A board that evaluates itself regularly, learns from others, shares ideas, and finds ways to continuously improve its own performance.

"We have an excellent school board. Every single board member is in it for the right reasons—first and foremost for the kids in the district. That's what makes us so cohesive," says Stothert. "We're not without our disagreements, but we all have the same goal. And I think that makes it absolutely a joy. We all respect each other, and the strategic plan drives us and keeps us focused. We know what we have to do, and we know where we need to be in five years. We all feel passionately that we can get the work completed."

The work of continuous improvement started in 1990, when Millard first turned to strategic planning. The district worked with the Cambridge Group, a consulting firm founded by Bill Cook that is widely known for helping school systems create a community-based and results-oriented strategic planning process. The key components of the process are:

- Direct involvement of stakeholders;
- Action plans that become part of principals' and central office administrators' job accountability requirements and annual evaluations;
- Objectives that focus on student achievement outcomes;
- Strategies that make it possible to attain district and school objectives; and
- Annual updates and periodic renewals.

The district sent several district administrators for training in the Cambridge model and, within a year, used this trained administrative corps to help put in place a site-based version of the district's strategic planning model in every school building. The strategic plan led to the development of the Millard Educational Program, which uses clearly defined and measurable standards to ensure that all students learn the academic and life skills necessary for success. Strategic planning also led to all-day kindergartens and advancements in the use of technology for learning. In 1997, Millard voters approved an $89 million bond issue—the largest ever passed in the state at that time—to construct new schools, remodel existing ones, and provide technology in every school.

The strategic planning process was just the beginning of a continuing cycle of analysis and re-evaluation. During an intensive two-day retreat in 1999, Millard's Strategic Planning Committee met to review the district's strengths and weaknesses and to analyze the impact of population shifts, economic and social trends, and technological developments. Using that information, the committee reached a consensus on mission and belief statements for the district and developed six overarching strategies for accomplishing the mission. The school board approved the draft in August 1999 and shared it with the community, which was invited to participate in the next step—developing action plans. For the next three months, nearly 100 volunteers worked on defining ways to achieve the strategies, and in November the teams presented 29 plans to the Strategic Planning Committee. The committee accepted most of the action plans, modified others, and rejected a few that were not directly related to the intent of the stated strategy. In January 2000 the board approved the strategic plan as a dynamic working document.

In Millard, continuous improvement means envisioning and preparing for the future, so in 2003 district leaders held an intensive three-day retreat to prepare a new five-year plan. A core group of 33 people (including high school students, teachers, and members of the community in addition to board members, the superintendent, and members of his executive committee) revisited the mission statement and the school system's beliefs and initiated the process of developing strategies and action plans. The retreat "is really an environmental scan," says Superintendent Keith Lutz. "We examine our strengths and weaknesses, drawing on data as well as on the perceptions of people at the table." In this model, each member of the committee has an equal voice.

"Our decisions are made not by voting but by consensus," explains Stothert. "We agree at the beginning that whatever we agree on and put down on paper, we will all strongly and passionately support." The committee crafted a new mission statement, eight new strategies, and, with the help of 200 community and staff members, drew up 53 new action plans over a four-month period. The school board approved the strategic plan in March 2004. "Some of the action plans carry a little more urgency," says Stothert. "We have a timetable of what we hope to achieve and when."

Responding to Changing Needs

As it begins its quest to become a world-class district, the school board finds itself faced with the first test of its resolve—rallying community support for a bond issue that will raise money to build and renovate schools to meet the district's population growth. The district enrolled 420 new students in the 2003-04 school year and another 500 in 2004-05. "Subdivisions are going up like wildfire," says Stothert. "We have 4,500 lots being developed within the district's boundary lines [that] have not yet been assigned to schools—that's a huge number of potential students."

To serve these students, the district must build new schools. One elementary school will open in 2005, and Stothert says the district is buying land for another school. A fourth high school may be needed, along with a facility to house the district's technology programs, which are currently located at a middle school that is fast reaching capacity. A possible redesign of the district's alternative education programs may result in greater facilities needs. To pay for new construction, the district will ask voters to pass a bond issue, whose size has not yet been determined.

"We have a five-year plan to deal with growth," explains Stothert. "Our superintendent is extremely visionary and excellent at planning for the future and for what our district needs. And we are driven in the same direction. We have promised to keep achievement high and class size low and to be responsible with our money, but we cannot wait until kids are falling out the windows to start building new schools."

A few years ago, a telephone survey of the community (nonparents as well as parents) gauged interest in another form of support for the schools—a tax-levy override to allow the district to increase its resources for programs and buildings. A private polling company conducted 10-minute interviews of 500 people, using a random sample the district provided. The Millard Education Foundation funded the project. Although voters had passed every bond issue in the past, they expressed considerably less interest in overriding a cap on taxes. Taking the survey's advice, the district has decided not to call a special election to ask voters for permission to exceed the tax-levy cap.

Now, however, attitudes toward spending more money on schools are definitely changing. Earlier, for example, voters in the southwest corner of the district did not support building a new school, but as the school population continues to swell in that area, those same people are asking when the district will build more schools. "The growth has been such that, within a year, there are hardly any plots of land left we can even buy to build a school," Stothert says. "People are feeling the pinch more, with the high schools at maximum enrollment and class sizes increasing."

What concerns Stothert and the other board members is the fact that only 38 percent of Millard's population has children in school. "It's that larger group of people who don't have kids in school anymore that we have to convince that this is the thing to do," she says. "A lot of them are saying, 'I don't have kids—this is not my problem.' We will have to engage the community enough to sell the idea that people will have to pay more taxes if they want to maintain quality."

Stothert says the board has done a really good job of maintaining fiscal responsibility. The district refinanced its old bonds and got an increase in its bond rating—almost unheard of in a public school district. "We have managed our money carefully and been under budget in almost everything we have done," she adds. "We have a cash reserve. We've done a good job but cannot keep building schools without new money."

To get that message across, the board and administration are developing an entire marketing plan, putting time, thought, and effort into determining how to market the new mission statement and the bond issue, which are tied together, and how to describe the district's aspirations to the community. The district's communications director has created an award-winning school calendar, Stothert says, and a "great poster in every classroom in every school with our new mission statement and pictures of the board of education. We think we have what it takes to get to the next level."

Communicating Expectations for the District

As it presents its case for a world-class system to the community, the school board will draw on its solid history of communicating with the public. The six-member board—with all members elected at large—sets and communicates direction through various publications, through the Millard website, and through multiple town hall meetings. Community participation is encouraged at the district's three to four monthly board meetings. Two are regularly scheduled formal meetings, and two are informal sessions that allow for more discussion on a limited number of agenda items.

The town hall meetings differ from regular, formal board meetings in that the audience is encouraged to give feedback to the board about district programs and policies. For several years, the board as a whole went to each of the district's five middle schools for town hall meetings. Now, it holds the meetings at each of the school system's three high schools. The meetings are well received and well attended—often attracting a standing-room-only crowd of 300-400 people, says Stothert. "We want to tell people what's going on and, more important, to hear back from them," she says. "We tell them that if we can't answer [a question], we will find someone who can. We've made a real effort to be part of the community and to try to be the link between the community and the school district." The board plans to use the town hall meetings to present the new mission statement and strategic plan. It will also spread its message at Parent-Teacher Organization meetings. Each year, too, the district has a "welcome back" event for the entire teaching staff, which gives the board a chance to explain the mission and action plans and to inspire teachers. "All this is helping to get the message out." Stothert says.

"Communication is so vital," she adds. "You think you are doing a good job, but then you go to a town hall meeting and you realize people have not understood the issues. They might say, 'We are paying more money in taxes. Where is our money going?' So we explain, in simple terms, the budget and where the monies come from to run the public schools."

Within the past two years, state aid has been cut $9 million, but the school district still managed to take in 420 new students with no additional staff. "We have managed to remain a high-achieving, low-spending school district," Stothert says. "We are the third-lowest spending in the whole area, including Lincoln. We have done a pretty good job with our money."

The town meetings at the high school have been particularly revealing when students ask hard questions, she says: "You really have your eyes opened by students. They are concerned with things that directly affect them—codes of conduct, dress codes. 'Why do we get in trouble when we wear a hooded sweatshirt to school?' 'Why do we have so many assessments?' A lot of times they think we are there to make their lives miserable, but once we explain federal and state requirements and why we raised the requirements to graduate, they can accept it."

Students are included in strategic planning as well, and the school district has made major changes based on their ideas and feedback. Stothert recalls that when the district wanted to require five credits of fine arts and five credits of technology education, the students said they already had developed skills that took them well beyond the material taught at school. "And it was true," Stothert says. Because of students' comments, the district reviewed its technology curriculum and added more classes.

The school board also understands that revising its policies is an important part of strategic planning and continuous improvement. Because many board policies had not been reviewed for 20 years, they were out of date and sometimes out of touch with community needs. Stothert says policy review is now a part of every regularly scheduled board meeting: "Our goal is to review every policy at least once every seven years, so we have 70-80 policies to update or reaffirm each year." The administrator concerned with a particular issue redrafts the relevant board policy, and the school system's attorney reviews it before it goes to the board for a first reading. The board reads the policy out loud, discusses it, suggests any necessary changes, and brings it back to the next regularly scheduled meeting for approval.

Improving the Board's Own Operations

The board formally evaluates its own performance and also sets goals for its own improvement. These goals address topics such as policy development, curriculum and assessment alignment, involvement in and influence on legislative activity, and resource allocation. They are in addition to goals set for the superintendent and the student achievement goals of the strategic plan, which are, of course, board goals as well. "We evaluate ourselves as a group," Stothert adds. "We don't go after individual members. The camaraderie is absolutely wonderful. We have developed such respect for each other and have learned from each other even though we don't always agree."

Once a year, the board reviews the policies that govern it, to remind board members of their roles. "We all feel very strongly that our role is policy making and that Dr. Lutz runs the district. We hired him to run the school district. He's the educational expert. We are the policy makers and the link between the community and the school district," Stothert says.

"We as a board are always trying to improve," she adds. The board is committed to continuing education, and to learning from others and sharing its ideas. For six out of the last eight years, the Millard school board received the "outstanding board" award from the Nebraska Association of School Boards (NASB). Board members attend the annual National School Boards Association Annual Conference, which they use as a team-building exercise. Stothert represents Millard on a regional group, the Metropolitan Area Boards of Education, which includes 10 districts that meet monthly and share ideas on everything from board and superintendent evaluations to reading or alternative education programs. The meetings, facilitated by a representative from NASB, are held in a different district each month. Although the participating school districts are of different sizes and face different issues, Stothert says she believes they are all in the same boat and should cooperate rather than compete.

The board also evaluates the superintendent on the progress of the strategic plan, his leadership skills, and his knowledge of the curriculum. In addition, it sets additional goals for Lutz, who can earn a bonus for achieving them. For example, says Stothert, "we wanted him to be more of a presence in school buildings and to be more available to staff." As a result, Lutz set up more sessions with staff members so they can ask him questions.

The superintendent has met every goal the board set for him, Stothert says. He made a great effort to hold parent coffees and forums not only with parents and staff but with students as well. He has also been active in community organizations such as the Rotary and Omaha2000.

The school board has developed an excellent working relationship with Lutz, who Stothert says has a passion for education. "Just as a joke, I started calling the superintendent 'Dad' one day," she says. While they would never address him this way at a board meeting or in public, sometimes, among themselves, board members might ask, "Where's Dad? What does Dad want us to do with this?" As Stothert says, "We are comfortable with him, but he is extremely professional, he has a lot of integrity, and we trust him. That makes the relationship great. You know exactly how he feels and vice versa. We know exactly where we stand."

Lutz has helped teach the board the fine art of responding to criticism in a constructive way. "Our superintendent takes criticism extremely well. In fact, he asks for it," Stothert says. Lutz has gone to every school and met with representative teachers at every site. "At first we thought, 'You are just setting yourself up, you'll have criticism, you'll be yelled at,' but he said, 'No, I want it, I want to hear what they have to say,'" Stothert reports. "He responds in a way that is not defensive. He is always very calm. Any controversial subject, he will hold a forum. But he's great at saying 'This is my meeting, and I will set the ground rules.'"

As an example of Lutz's ability to listen well and defuse issues, Stothert cites his handling of parents involved with the Core Academy, an elementary school that provides a good deal of structure—one of the many programs of choice the district allows because it believes that children learn in different ways. (District policies permit each building to do its own site-based planning as long as the plan is aligned with the district's strategic plan. Although individual schools may choose various ways to educate children, all children are expected to pass the same districtwide assessments.)

The parents wanted a "core" middle school as well as a component for gifted students, although the school's initial blueprint said the academic program was rigorous enough without special attention to gifted students. Many parents were angry, but Superintendent Lutz listened and was not defensive, Stothert recalls. In fact, he said he would help concerned parents form a committee to study whether to rewrite the guidelines for the program and redo the plan, which requires the development of a cost-benefit analysis and numerous other steps taken over a 15-18 month period. The committee will bring its recommendations back to the superintendent, who will bring them to the board.

While it encourages variety and diversity, the district also makes clear what is not acceptable. "We had one building that wanted to try year-round schooling, but that was not a new program," Stothert explains. That was a calendar change, which only the district can initiate.

Measuring Students' Mastery of Skills

The centerpiece of Millard's continuous improvement plan has been its strategy for student mastery of academic skills in reading, mathematics, writing, science, and social science. This strategy involves a system of student assessments, called the Millard Essential Learner Outcomes (ELOs)—criterion-referenced assessments that district students must master to graduate from high school—coupled with remediation for those students who do not achieve mastery on the first attempt. For more than 10 years, the ELOs have been used to indicate the degree to which the district is achieving its mission of having all students acquire necessary academic skills.

The school years are divided into primary, intermediate, middle school, and high school blocks. Within each block, assessments in writing, reading, mathematics, science, and social science are given at different times. The achievement of mastery or proficiency of any ELO assessment is noted by a "cut score"—a score established by groups of district teachers who participated in rigorous standard-setting workshops and by testing experts at the University of Nebraska. Students who do not score at or above the cutoffs are involved in various remediation strategies and are reassessed in the ELO content areas.

Clearly, the district has made major strides toward its goal of having 100 percent of students master the ELOs. In most grades and content areas, the percent of students attaining the ELO standards is 95 to 99 percent. One incentive for success has been the district's Career Compensation Model, which gives building-wide bonuses to schools that show growth in ELO performance. A school's ELO indicator is obtained by averaging percent mastery across grades and content areas. The model is designed to reward schools that have a newly calculated three-year average that exceeds the prior three-year average, or that have an overall new three-year average that is greater than 90 percent mastery, on initial testing, without reteaching or retesting.

During the 2002-03 school year, every school reached its goal for the first time, says Lutz. The district rewarded school personnel with a total of $550,000, which included a donation of $190,000 from the Millard Education Foundation and a school system contribution of $360,000. Each teacher received $400, and each classified staff member (such as cook or custodian) received $200. "Every staff member is important to the mission," says Lutz. "All have a role to play with kids." The district website and the Nebraska State Department of Education website publish results of the ELO assessments. Standardized test results are also published on the district site and are presented at the school and district level in an annual statistical profile.

The office of Planning, Evaluation, and Information Services has an online intranet in place that allows administrators to disaggregate data for subgroups and to list students' test scores in areas they have not mastered. Those results are used for goal setting and for planning at the school and district levels.

"We leave nothing to chance," says Lutz. "We use data to drive all our decisions. We try to measure everything that moves around here."

The data is clear, easy to understand, and easy to communicate to others, says Stothert. "We get the data that we ask for. In math, for example, if we want to see the trend from the fourth to the fifth to the sixth grade, we get it. Dr. Crawford [executive director of planning and evaluation] is more than accommodating—his data is understandable, and we know what to do with it."

The board discusses data regularly and uses it to revise or realign the curriculum and to be certain the written curriculum is actually the curriculum that is being taught and tested. One concern is with Advanced Placement (AP) classes. Because the district does not require students to take AP exams, it has no real way to know whether teachers are actually teaching the AP curriculum. "One of our goals is to make sure the AP curriculum is aligned with AP exams," says Stothert. "We want to make sure that when students take an AP course, they are truly taking an AP course."

Each year, the district produces an annual report that is printed as a supplement to the *Omaha World Herald*. The report details the sources of school funds and how they are spent and publishes test results and trends over the last 10 years. "The annual report is well read. People tell me they wish other districts would do such a good job," Stothert says.

Teacher training is another important instructional focus. The teacher evaluation system has been recently overhauled to reflect the board's and superintendent's focus on continuous improvement. The system includes a cycle in which teachers set professional goals and then evaluate whether their students' performance has improved as a result of their teaching. Teachers are also required to have two full days of training in the differentiation of instruction and one full day in technology integration. The training, for which teachers receive payment on a per-diem rather than an hourly basis, takes place outside the regular school day and regular staff development days. "The [differentiation of instruction] training was fairly costly, but it was one of the better things we have done," says Lutz. "It took us three years to cycle through the first training cycle, and now we are in part two."

Determining Customer Satisfaction

The superintendent continually teaches administrators about "customer focus"—who the school system's customers are and how best to serve a community of many different customer-stakeholders. Central office administrators consider teachers and all other building staff their customers, and all staff and administrators consider students and the community their customers. "We are all good listeners," Lutz says.

For her part, Stothert prefers the term "partners." "We say we have a partnership with the students, the parents, the community, and the staff," she says. "We say we are all in this together. We believe that all these people have a stake and a voice. We are always seeking the voice of the community."

To determine the stakeholders' satisfaction, the district uses a locally developed effective schools questionnaire each year to survey parents, students in grades five through 12, certified staff, and support staff members. In the parent survey, for example, a random sample of about 20 percent of district parents are asked a variety of questions about safety and behavior, curriculum, and administrative issues. The survey's return rate is generally from 45 to 55 percent.

A key survey question is, "What grade would you give your school(s)?" The board perceives the answer as an evaluation of its performance and parents' satisfaction with the whole system. The number of parents giving an A or B rating has risen to 93 percent in recent years, while national suburban percentages are around 70 percent. These results and other survey findings are given to principals and central office staff to use in site-based planning and district strategic planning.

Both the school board and superintendent have been recognized at the state and national level for leadership in implementing innovative programs in strategic planning and using assessments to improve student learning. Each year, the board and the superintendent and his staff make presentations at state and national conferences, sharing their strategies and getting feedback from other education professionals.

Perhaps the best indicator that the community believes its board is doing a good job is board members' high re-election rate. Since 1990, a total of 14 of 17 board members (82 percent) have been elected to at least two four-year terms.

The school district is continually involved in a cycle of measurement, implementation, evaluation, and measurement. "We have been true to our strategic planning process and have stuck to it over the years," says Lutz. "It's been the driving force for all our change efforts, and the ultimate result has been higher achievement." His advice to other districts is to persist even in the face of fatigue and to continue to work for change.

Stothert says communication remains the key. "Listen to the community and learn to communicate better with the public," she advises. "And evaluate yourself as a board and take those extra steps to make your [functioning] better." She also urges school board members to take the post for the right reason—for the kids. "Good school board members do not come in with a single agenda," she says. "They care about the kids and what the kids can achieve."

For more information:
John Crawford
Executive Director of Planning and Evaluation
Millard Public Schools
5606 S. 147th St.
Omaha, NE 68137
Telephone: (402) 895-8214
E-mail: jcrawford@mpsomaha.org
The district's website is www.mpsomaha.org.

Signs of Success

The following results are indicators of the Millard school district's commitment to continuous improvement:

- Millard's scores on the American College Testing (ACT) assessment are consistently above regional, state, and national averages. In 2002, Millard's average ACT score was 22.7 on a scale of 1 to 35, compared with 21.5 (metro), 21.7 (state), and 20.8 (nation).

- Students perform at exemplary levels and far exceed the state's average scores in all grade levels tested on the State Report Card.

- On the Terra Nova Achievement Test, students scored above the 70th national percentile in almost all subjects. Results for fall 2002, comparing the same cohort of students across grades three and four, showed that students made large gains in reading (+8 points), with moderate gains in language and social studies (+4 points each). The total battery score showed these students increasing from the 73rd to the 78th percentile.

- The school district has earned the state's highest accreditation rating, and six Millard schools have been winners in the U.S. Department of Education's "Blue Ribbon Schools" program to recognize exemplary schools.

CONTINUOUS IMPROVEMENT RESOURCES

Baldrige National Quality Program; Education Criteria for Performance
Excellence. www.baldrige.nist.gov/Education_Criteria.htm.
> Malcolm Baldrige was a proponent of quality management as a key to
> America's prosperity and long-term strength. The Baldrige Award is given
> by the president of the United States to businesses, education organiza-
> tions, and health care organizations that apply and are judged to be out-
> standing in seven criteria. The education version of the Baldrige Criteria
> was created in the mid-1990s as a framework for understanding and
> improving school performance and student learning. The criteria provide
> the basis for assessment and feedback, creating a foundation for continu-
> ous improvement. They are built upon a set of interrelated core values
> and concepts that characterize all types of high-performing organizations,
> as well as highly successful schools and school districts.

Bolman, Lee G., and Terrence E. Deal. *Reframing Organizations: Artistry, Choice,
and Leadership.* (3rd ed.) Jossey-Bass, 2003. 483 pp.
> The authors provide leaders and managers with new perspectives (frames)
> to understand and manage organizations. The book teaches managers and
> leaders how to reframe experience from different perspectives, using
> structural, human resource, political, and symbolic types of frames as
> tools to help leaders adapt to a constantly changing environment.

Clemson University. *Public Sector Continuous Improvement Guide.*
http://deming.eng.clemson.edu/pub/psci.
> This detailed website contains links to a wide variety of resources on con-
> tinuous improvement, total quality management, and related management
> concepts that can be applied to agencies and organizations in the public
> sector.

Collins, Jim. *Good to Great: Why Some Companies Make the Leap—and Others Don't.*
HarperBusiness, 2001. 300 pp.
> A "prequel" to the author's bestseller *Built to Last*, this book explores the
> ways good organizations can be turned into great ones that produce
> exceptional, sustained results. Collins and his team of researchers exam-
> ined more than 1,400 Fortune 500 companies, finally settling on 11 that
> met the authors' criteria for making substantial improvements over time.
> They then identified the common traits of these great companies.

Collins, Jim, and Jerry I. Porras. *Built to Last: Successful Habits of Visionary Companies.* HarperBusiness Essentials, 2002. 342 pp.

> The result of a six-year research project at the Stanford University Graduate School of Business, *Built to Last* identifies 18 "visionary" companies and analyzes the keys to their success. The companies included had to be world famous, have a stellar brand image, and be at least 50 years old. These companies were then compared to a control group of somewhat less successful competitor companies to answer the question, What makes the truly exceptional, long-lasting companies different from other companies?

Covey, Stephen R. *The Seven Habits of Highly Effective People: Restoring the Character Ethic.* Simon and Schuster, 1989. 340 pp.

> Leadership authority Stephen Covey spells out a best-selling prescription for personal and professional success based on seven positive principles that have stood the test of time.

Ginsburg, Alan, Andrew Lauland, and Natalia Pane. *Continuous Improvement Management Guide for 21st Century Schools.* 1999. PowerPoint presentation available at www.ed.gov/offices/OUS/PES/21cent/improve.pdf.

> Setting measurable goals and ongoing self-assessment are critical for ensuring that an educational program is meeting its objectives and having a positive impact on the community it serves. To illustrate these principles, the Department of Education developed this summary PowerPoint presentation about the continuous improvement management process for schools. (See related book version under Pane, Natalia.)

Goldberg, Jacqueline S., and Bryan R. Cole. "Quality Management in Education: Building Excellence and Equity in Student Performance." *Quality Management Journal,* vol. 9 no. 4, October 2002. Available at www.asq.org/pub/qmj/past/vol9_issue4/qmjv9i4goldberg.pdf.

> This article describes a research project based on a study of Brazosport Independent School District in Texas, where a quality management approach resulted in greater equity and higher student performance. In a yearlong qualitative study of Brazosport ISD, the researchers analyzed and documented the approach and deployment of quality management and analyzed the outcomes and implications for continuous improvement.

Grand Prize Winner: Continuous Improvement. Finley School District No. 53, Kennewick, Washington. *Magna Awards 2001*, supplement to *American School Board Journal*, April 2001, p. A4.

> Beginning in 1998, the Finley School Board initiated a Comprehensive Cultural Improvement Advocacy Program. Its objective was "to promote the active development of the entire Finley learning community toward a vision of a 'learner organization' and to continually improve the conditions of learning for students." Before the end of the program's first year, the school board had involved the entire community, including students and staff, in comprehensive strategic planning. The group determined that student achievement would *not* be the main focus of the program; instead, they felt that improved learning would happen if the right environment could be provided. The program has succeeded in part because it looks at all elements of the education experience as a comprehensive system.

Hawley, Willis D., and Donald L. Rollie. *The Keys to Effective Schools: Educational Reform as Continuous Improvement*. Corwin Press (co-published with the National Education Association), 2002. 128 pp.

> After several years of surveying teachers and school staff and comparing their answers to actual student test results, National Education Association researchers identified 42 characteristics common to high-achieving schools. In this NEA KEYS Initiative (Keys to Excellence for Your Schools) publication, top experts in school reform present steps to solve organizational problems that limit student achievement.

McKenzie-Wilson, Karen. "An Incredible Journey: Tools for Continuous Improvement." *Multimedia Schools*, vol. 9 no. 6, Nov/Dec 2002. Pages 20-23. Available at www.infotoday.com/mmschools/nov02/mckenzie-wilson.htm.

> Describes the significant improvements in student performance achieved through the application of the process of continuous improvement in the Plano Independent School District, Plano, Texas. The article provides a detailed view of the tools and concepts employed for success in this school district setting.

National School Boards Foundation. *Improving School Board Decision-Making: The Data Connection.* NSBF, 2002. 92 pages. Available for purchase from the National School Boards Association publications ordering service, (800) 706-6722.

> This straightforward guidebook explains how school board members can identify the appropriate data to inform their decisions, work with the superintendent to analyze and interpret the data, use the data to support the board's policy and budget decisions, and inform the community about the meaning and significance of school district data.

Pane, Natalia, Ivor Mulligan, Alan Ginsburg, and Andrew Lauland. *A Guide to Continuous Improvement Management (CIM) for 21st Century Community Learning Centers.* U.S. Department of Education, February 1999. 101 pages. Available at www.ed.gov/offices/OUS/PES/21cent/cim226.pdf.

> This guide to Continuous Improvement Management (CIM) explains the guiding principles and the process of CIM in a detailed, but clearly written and accessible format. Specific examples are cited throughout for basic processes such as stock-taking, setting objectives, and assessing and reporting outcomes.

Rudy, Dennis W,. and William H. Conrad. "Breaking Down the Data." *American School Board Journal,* February 2004, pp. 39-41. Available at www.asbj.com/2004/02/0204asbjrudy.pdf.

> The authors served as consultants to the District Data Use Project, an initiative sponsored by the American Association of School Administrators, the National School Boards Foundation, and UCLA's National Center for Research on Standards and Student Testing (CRESST). More than 50 school districts enhanced the power of data-driven decision making through web-based Quality School Portfolio (QSP) software and other support tools from CRESST. As part of the project's work, school board members were interviewed about the effective uses of data for continuous improvement.

Senge, Peter M. *The Fifth Discipline: The Art and Practice of the Learning Organization.* Doubleday/Currency, 1994, 1990. 423 pp.

> In applying systems thinking to business success, Senge defines five business "disciplines" that help to build "learning organizations," which are "organizations where people continually expand their capacity to create the results they truly desire, where new and expansive patterns of think-

ing are nurtured, where collective aspiration is set free, and where people are continually learning how to learn together." The author is the founder of the Center for Organizational Learning at MIT's Sloan School of Management.

Senge, Peter M., and others. *The Fifth Discipline Fieldbook: Strategies and Tools for Building a Learning Organization.* Doubleday/Currency, 1994. 593 pp.
> While Senge's *Fifth Discipline* lays out the principles for long-term organizational improvement, his *Fifth Discipline Fieldbook* is meant to answer the question, "What should we do differently when we go to work on Monday morning?" Drawing on the experiences of an entire community of practitioners, the book describes how to get started in the practice of the principles of organizational learning.

Senge, Peter M., and others. *The Dance of Change: The Challenges of Sustaining Momentum in Learning Organizations.* Doubleday/Currency, 1999. 642 pp.
> *The Dance of Change* is a fieldbook of strategies and methods for moving beyond the first steps of corporate change and generating long-lasting results. Written by the *Fifth Discipline Fieldbook* team, it provides insider perspectives on the challenges of implementing learning and change initiatives in major international corporations.

Senge, Peter M., and others. *Schools That Learn: A Fifth Discipline Fieldbook for Parents, Educators, and Everyone Who Cares about Education.* Doubleday/Currency, 2000. 592 pp.
> *Schools That Learn* applies the theories, tools, and methods of organizational learning developed in the *Fifth Discipline* books to our system of education. Instead of presenting quick fixes for the current problems with our schools, this approach is designed to understand and influence the underlying forces that shape schools and communities for the long haul.

Togneri, Wendy, and Stephen E. Anderson. *Beyond Islands of Excellence: What Districts Can Do to Improve Instruction and Achievement in All Schools: A Leadership Brief.* Learning First Alliance, 2003. 16 pp. www.learningfirst.org/publications/districts.
> A study by the Learning First Alliance demonstrates how five high-poverty school districts raised student achievement by focusing on district-wide strategies to improve instruction. This summary report outlines seven

findings from the five districts and identifies practical steps school districts can take to move beyond a few excellent schools to success across entire systems.

Walton, Mary. *The Deming Management Method.* Perigree Books (Putnam), 1988. 262 pp.
> A very readable summary of W. Edwards Deming's life and his revolutionary management methods. Deming's theories embrace change that starts at the top with informed, quality-conscious management; they also emphasize employee involvement and continuous improvement throughout the organization.

Wheatley, Margaret J. *Leadership and the New Science: Discovering Order in a Chaotic World.* (rev. and expanded ed.) Berrett-Koehler and McGraw-Hill, 2000. 215 pp.
> In her bestselling *Leadership and the New Science*, Wheatley showed how revolutionary discoveries in quantum physics, chaos theory, and biology—which are overturning traditional images of the universe—can provide powerful insights into the design, leadership, and management of organizations. In the revised and expanded second edition of her work, she includes examples of applications of these ideas in organizations all over the world. Striking scientific photos enhance the book.

Wisconsin Successful School Guide: Continuous School Improvement Website. www.dpi.state.wi.us/sig/improvement/index.html.
> The Wisconsin Information Network for Successful Schools is an electronic resource created to help education leaders, parents, and community members find key local, state, and national information about successes in education. It was created through a partnership of the North Central Regional Education Laboratory, the Office of the Governor, and the Department of Public Instruction. The Continuous School Improvement website links to information about the characteristics of a successful school, sample school improvement planning tools, tips for building strong school improvement teams, and sample survey instruments for student and staff surveys.

Zmuda, Allison, Robert Kuklis, and Everett Kline. *Transforming Schools: Creating a Culture of Continuous Improvement.* Association for Supervision and Curriculum Development, 2004. 195 pp.

> This book approaches the transformation of schools by placing primary emphasis on learning and by regarding schools as competent systems in the long-term process of educational change. The first chapter outlines the six steps of continuous improvement needed to move toward a competent system in which everyone performs better as a result of a collective endeavor. The remaining chapters discuss the steps of continuous improvement in greater detail. Principles are illustrated through fictional settings throughout the book.

Compiled by the NSBA Library, October 2004

About the Authors

Katheryn W. Gemberling is an independent educational consultant who works with school boards and school district leadership throughout the country on topics related to improving student achievement. She specializes in training principals and other educators on data-driven decision making to improve student results. Previously she served for 32 years in Montgomery County (Md.) Public Schools as a teacher, principal, associate superintendent, and deputy superintendent. She earned a bachelor's degree from Ohio Wesleyan and a master's in mathematics from American University. Kathy and her husband live in Silver Spring, Md. They have one son.

Carl W. Smith is the executive director of the Maryland School Boards Association (MABE). In that role, he works closely with boards of education and board members across Maryland, promoting local school governance and the leadership role of boards of education. He has held a variety of leadership roles in public education, including teacher, principal, director, associate superintendent with the Montgomery County (Md). Public Schools and superintendent of the Brandywine School District in North Wilmington, Del. Before coming to MABE, he was an associate professor of education and coordinator of the Educational Leadership Program at Bridgewater State College in Massachusetts. He earned a bachelor's degree in education from Rhode Island College and a master's in history and a Ph.D. in educational administration from the University of Maryland, College Park. Carl and his wife live in Columbia, Md. They have three adult children.

Joseph S. Villani is deputy executive director of the National School Boards Association (NSBA). He previously served for 26 years in Montgomery County (Md.) Public Schools as a teacher, principal, director, and associate superintendent. He earned a bachelor's degree from St. Vincent College, a master's degree from the University of Pittsburgh, and a Ph.D. in human development from the University of Maryland. Joe and his wife live in Germantown, Md. They have three children.

Judith Brody Saks is a freelance writer in Rockville, Md., who writes frequently on education. The former executive director of Washington Independent Writers and a former senior editor of *American School Board Journal*, Judy has contributed to numerous NSBA publications, including *The Community Connection: Case Studies in Public Engagement*.

Other Titles in NSBA's Key Work of School Boards Series

Aligning Resources for Student Achievement, by A. Bruce McKay and Joanne Newcombe. 2002. 48 pages. This publication provides a way of thinking about how the resources available in a school district can be best used for raising student achievement. It is designed to give school boards concrete examples of alignment processes in each of the board's major roles, suggestions for clarifying the superintendent and staff roles and responsibilities, and questions to ask during the year to ensure the alignment of all aspects of resources in the district. (List price $15. National Affiliate Member price $12.) Order item **09-142**.

The Key Work of School Boards Guidebook, by Katheryn W. Gemberling, Carl W. Smith, and Joseph S. Villani. 2000. 95 pp. This guidebook provides information for understanding and implementing the Key Work of School Boards. It is intended as a support to help school boards understand and achieve the essential elements of their work. The guidebook provides a framework of eight key action areas that successful boards have focused their attention on: vision, standards, assessment, accountability, resource alignment, climate, collaboration, and continuous improvement. It is offered as a resource to help boards of education carry out their responsibilities for creating equity and excellence in public education and for leading the community in preparing all students to succeed in a rapidly changing global society. List price $20. National Affiliate Member price $16. Order item **09-140.**

Team Leadership for Student Achievement, by Ellen Henderson, Jeannie Henry, Judith Brody Saks, and Anne Wright. 211 pages. This publication is intended to serve as a stimulus for dialogue, an inspiration for building relationships, and a framework for mutually developed teamwork between the school board and the superintendent. It is not a code of rules to be followed point by point, thereby further compartmentalizing boards and superintendents into static roles and fixed relationships. Rather, it is based on a systems approach to addressing issues and making decisions through ongoing dialogue and reflection as needs and circumstances change. 2001. 211 pages. (List price $20; National Affiliate Member price $16.) Order item **09-141.**

OTHER PUBLICATIONS AVAILABLE FROM THE NATIONAL SCHOOL BOARDS ASSOCIATION

Becoming a Better Board Member (300+pp.), a comprehensive guide to board service and NSBA's most widely read book. Appropriate for both new and veteran school board members. Keeps school boards up to date on the issues affecting public education. (List price $21; National Affiliate Member price $16.80.) Order item **01-103-GE**.

The Community Connection: Case Studies in Public Engagement (68 pp.) reports case studies of 15 school districts nationwide that have engaged their communities to improve student achievement. Examines trends and frameworks emerging from the district studies, including how to define roles and provide for balanced community representation. Offers detailed district profiles, creative ideas, and practical solutions. Includes list of resources for engaging the community to raise student achievement. (List price $20; NSBA National Affiliate Member price $16) Order item **04-119-GE**.

Communities Count: A School Board Guide to Community Engagement (35 pp.) guides school board members through the community engagement process. Discusses the rationale, benefits, and concerns associated with convening the community. Examines the school board's leadership role in public engagement; presents strategies for focus groups and polling; identifies publications and Internet resources for further information. (List price $20; NSBA National Affiliate Member price $16) Order item **11-125-GE**.

Raising the Bar: A School Board Primer on Student Achievement (56 pp.) links the school board's leadership role to student achievement. Provides knowledge for effective decision making, processes and activities that enhance the school board's leadership role, and information sources. A fundamental reference tool for local school board members. (List price $20; NSBA National Affiliate Member price $16) Order item **11-121-GE**.

Reaching for Excellence: What Local School Districts are Doing to Raise Student Achievement (84 pp.) reports on survey of stratified random sample of 2,000 urban, suburban, and rural school districts from across the nation. Discusses critical student achievement issues — leadership and accountability, standards, assessment, and factors that enable or hinder success. Translates issues into practice, presents successful district programs, identifies questions school boards need to ask and activities to pursue. (List price $20; NSBA National Affiliate Member price $16) Order item **04-118-GE**.

Reinventing School-Based Management: A School Board Guide to School-Based Improvement (66 pp.) examines school-based management (SBM) and reveals why this once-heralded educational reform has had limited payoff for students. Offers guidance for school boards and administrators for developing a new approach to school-based decision making through the school-based improvement (SBI) model. (List price $20; NSBA National Affiliate Member price $16). Order item **11-122-GE**.

To order, call NSBA at 1-800-706-6722.

Please have the item number and your credit card or purchase order information ready when you call. Shipping and handling charges additional.

About NSBA...

The National School Boards Association is a not-for-profit federation of state associations of school boards across the United States. Our mission is to foster excellence and equity in public education through school board leadership. We achieve that mission by representing the school board perspective before federal government agencies and with national organizations that affect education, and by providing vital information and services to state associations of school boards and local school boards throughout the nation.

NSBA advocates local school boards as the ultimate expression of grassroots democracy. NSBA supports the capacity of each school board—acting on behalf of and in close concert with the people of its community—to envision the future of education in its community, to establish a structure and environment that allow all students to reach their maximum potential, to provide accountability for the community on performance in the schools, and to serve as the key community advocate for children and youth and their public schools.

Founded in 1940, NSBA, through the Federation of State Associations, now represents 95,000 local school board members, virtually all of whom are elected. These local officials govern 14,890 local school districts serving the nation's more than 47 million public school students.

NSBA policy is determined by a 150-member Delegate Assembly of local school board members. The 25-member Board of Directors translates this policy into action. Programs and services are administered by the NSBA executive director and a 130-person staff. NSBA is located in metropolitan Washington, D.C.

National School Boards Association
1680 Duke Street
Alexandria, VA 22314-3493
Phone: (703) 838-6722
Fax: (703) 683-7590

Web Address: www.nsba.org. E-mail: info@nsba.org
Excellence and Equity in Public Education through School Board Leadership